WAIT FOR MARCY

Wait for Marcy

BY

ROSAMOND du JARDIN

AUTHOR OF "PRACTICALLY SEVENTEEN"

Image Cascade Publishing

MANUFACTURED IN THE UNITED STATES
OF AMERICA

A hardcover edition of this book was originally published by J. B. Lippincott Company. It is here reprinted by arrangement with HarperCollins Publishers.

First *Image Cascade Publishing* edition published 2003.

Library of Congress Cataloging in Publication Data
Du Jardin, Rosamond 1902-1963.
Wait for Marcy.

(Juvenile Girls)
Reprint. Originally published: New York & Philadelphia: J. B. Lippincott Company, 1950.

To my good friend,

ALICE RAITHEL

Books By Rosamond du Jardin

Tobey Heydon Books

Practically Seventeen (1949)
Class Ring (1951)
Boy Trouble (1953)
The Real Thing (1956)
Wedding in the Family (1958)
One of the Crowd (1961)

Marcy Rhodes Books:

Wait for Marcy (1950)
Marcy Catches Up (1952)
A Man for Marcy (1954)
Senior Prom (1957)

Pam & Penny Howard Books:

Double Date (1951)
Double Feature (1953)
Showboat Summer (1955)
Double Wedding (1959)

Non-Series Titles

Someone to Count on (1962)
Young and Fair (1963)
Junior Year Abroad (1960)

Adult Novels

All is Not Gold (1935)
Only Love Lasts (1937)
Honorable Estate (1943)
Brief Glory (1944)
Tomorrow Will Be Fair (1946)

WAIT FOR MARCY

Chapter One

THE WHITE FORMAL

Nothing was farther from Marcy Rhodes' mind, that May night, than the white net formal. She sat sprawled comfortably crosswise in a slip-covered chair, deeply engrossed in her favorite magazine. The white shirt she wore had long since been discarded by her father, her blue jeans were deeply cuffed. Floppy moccasins hung from her toes. At fifteen Marcy was dark and slim, with brown hair curled under in a soft bell. Hers were the sort of looks that might easily develop into real loveliness as she grew older. Marcy, however, would gladly have traded high cheek bones, wide dark eyes and golden tan skin for the blond, blue-eyed prettiness possessed by her closest friend, Liz Kendall.

"Marcy." The faint edge of insistence in her mother's tone hinted that she had spoken before. But certainly

Marcy hadn't heard her.

"What, Mom?"

She glanced across the pleasant, lamp-lit room at her mother, knitting on the couch. She was knitting a sweater for Marcy, a yellow sweater, the same shade as the forsythia that sprayed out like a delicate fountain from a low white bowl on the coffee table. Marcy's father sat in his favorite red leather chair near the windows, his nose deep in the evening paper. And Ken, her almost-seventeen-year-old brother, was so intent on a book at the desk that Marcy was sure it couldn't be any part of his homework. More likely it was one of the books on aeronautics he was always getting at the library. Never was a boy so crazy about airplanes as Ken.

"I was cleaning your closet today," Mom said, "and I came across that lovely dress Grandmother sent you."

"Oh, yes," Marcy breathed, her heart quickening just a little at the entrancing thought of it. "I always keep it in my garment bag, zipped up so it won't get dirty." She frowned, slightly anxious. "It was all right, wasn't it?"

"Yes," her mother's tone was dry, "quite all right."

Lila Rhodes was an agreeable-looking woman, just verging on plumpness, whose fair hair was only lightly frosted with gray. She had rather penetrating blue eyes and just now there was an expression in them that Marcy couldn't quite fathom, a sort of quizzically accusing look. But why, she wondered.

Marcy could remember, as clearly as if it were yesterday, Christmas morning when she had unwrapped the gift Gran had sent her from California. The dress she lifted from its sheltering nest of tissue was quite the most wonderful formal she had ever seen, its bodice so slim, its crisp net skirt so extravagantly wide and flecked lightly with silver like a scattered handful of stars.

"Just what I've dreamed of having," Marcy had crooned.

And she had rushed off upstairs, to return a little later garbed in the lovely dress, her hair tickling her bare shoulders, her fuzzy lamb's-wool bedroom slippers supplying a slightly incongruous note. But even they had not been able to detract greatly from the glamorous effect.

"Good Heavens, Marcy!" she distinctly recalled her father exclaiming. His eyes had widened incredulously behind his bi-focals, his mouth had dropped open just a little. And he had gasped, "Isn't it entirely too—too—"

"No," Marcy had denied, pirouetting before the mirror above the mantel, "it isn't too anything. It's perfect! Absolutely super-perfect!"

"Well, it's becoming all right," her father had admitted a trifle grudgingly. "But I don't know what Mother could have been thinking of! I mean—for a kid your age—" his tone had implied that something must have unhinged Gran's reason entirely.

"But, Daddy, all the girls have formals," Marcy had

objected. "Not such sharp ones as this, though! Gran is a dear, isn't she? I hardly hoped an old lady her age could pick out such a super-dress—"

"You mean," Mom had cut in, appalled, at this point, "you expected to get this particular gift from her?"

"Well"—Marcy wished, belatedly, that she had been a bit more careful in her choice of words—"I wasn't sure—"

"But why would you have even the slightest idea—unless—" her father had broken off then in obvious consternation.

And Mom had finished for him, equally aghast, but more vocal "—unless you had asked her to send you a party dress?"

Marcy had pleated the filmy folds of her lovely dress uneasily between her fingers. "Well—I did sort of ask her—but not in any objectionable way. You see," she had rushed on to explain, "Gran wrote me almost a month ago and asked me to send her a list of things I'd like for Christmas, so she'd have some idea what to get me, you know?"

Her mother had nodded, a smile beginning to tug at her lips. And Daddy had looked at least a few degrees less stern. Marcy had felt encouraged to continue. "So—I did. I told her six or seven different things and I explained that I'd be perfectly happy with any one of them. So I wasn't sure at all she'd get me a formal—" Marcy's eyes had crept back, fascinated, to her reflection in the mirror.

"And I certainly had no idea she'd pick out such a terrific one!"

It had been at this point that Ken, lifting his head belatedly from bemused contemplation of the plans of a model-plane kit, had seemed to become aware for the first time of what was going on around him. Startled admiration had glowed for an unguarded moment in his glance as he beheld Marcy. But he had got it under almost immediate control. "Wow!" he had said drily. "Never knew you had it in you, Revolting."

That had been Christmas morning. Now it was spring. And Mom, with that quizzically accusing look in her eye that baffled Marcy, inquired quietly, "When are you ever going to get around to wearing it?"

Apparently Daddy wasn't concentrating as deeply on the paper as he seemed to be. He lowered it to ask incredulously, "Hasn't she worn it yet, Lila? Why, it's been months!"

"I'll wear it sometime," Marcy said.

Parents could be awfully difficult. Even parents like hers, who, on the whole, were fairly reasonable. She wished her mother hadn't thought of cleaning closets today, then this whole issue might have been avoided.

She felt her father's glance, even more accusing than her mother's, fall heavily on her. "What's the idea, letting that dress hang around unworn all this time? After you told Mother you wanted it, and she went to all the trouble of getting it and sending it to you."

"I don't think she minded," Marcy said. "I imagine she got a bang out of buying something like that. It must get very dull always having to shop for matronly things, grays and lavenders." She looked from one of her parents to the other. Obviously, they weren't going to permit themselves to be side-tracked. Marcy sighed.

"But, dear," Mom objected above the faint brisk click of her knitting needles, "you'll outgrow it if you wait too long."

"I'm not growing any more—much," Marcy said. "It'll be okay." Older people could be so dense sometimes. She pointed out, "After all, you can't simply haul off and wear a dress like that just anywhere. It has to be some very special place, some important occasion."

Mom asked, a slight frown between her brows, "Couldn't you have worn it to some of the dances at school?"

"Oh, those!" Marcy tried for a note of scorn. It was disgusting to have her voice come out a little husky from having to force its way around the lump in her throat.

"Yeah," Ken spoke up with the utterly unfeeling candor of brothers and Marcy could have socked him. Why should he choose this particular time to shut his book and jump with both feet into a conversation that was certainly none of his business? "Yeah," Ken said, "but nobody asked Dream-puss to any of those."

"Don't call me that!" Marcy snapped at him.

Ken was a big, nice-looking boy, taller than their father, who was by no means short. He had toast-colored hair and blue eyes like Mom's, eyes that sometimes probed too deeply for comfort.

"Okay," Ken said with aggravating mildness. "But whatever I call you, it's still true nobody asked you to any of the dances."

"Ken, that's enough." Mom's tone was reproving. She looked at Marcy pityingly, as if she were sorry now that she had brought up the subject of the dress in the first place.

But Marcy didn't want pity. She wanted to hurt Ken, as his shrewd thrust had hurt her. Only she wouldn't give him the satisfaction of seeing that she cared.

She asked lightly, cuttingly, "Is that so? And I suppose all the smoothest girls at school are simply drooling over you!"

"Well, of course," Ken said, grinning his easy grin. "It's my charm and good looks and perfect manners."

It was hard to stay angry with Ken when he grinned like that. But the rage that comes from hurt is not quickly dispelled. Marcy said, "Some of those—those bags I see you with—"

"Now, see here." George Rhodes laid his paper aside with a little crackle. His tone was severe. "Didn't you both hear your mother say that was enough? I won't have you quarreling and being rude to each other."

"Well, he started it," Marcy said.

Ken objected, "All I said was—"

"We heard what you said." This was Mom, pouring oil on the troubled waters. "And we're not going to discuss the matter further."

"Okay," Ken agreed, shrugging. "But I don't see why she's so touchy."

"I'm not touchy!" Marcy denied hotly. "You're always picking on me!"

That wasn't, she realized even as she said it, quite true. It was a funny thing about brothers and sisters, or, at least, about Ken and herself. Ever since they were small, as long ago as Marcy could remember, there had been a kind of closeness between them, a feeling of understanding and kinship not to be denied. No matter how many fights they had, or how hotly they argued between themselves, there was ever that knowledge, deep down within, of being able to depend on each other. Back in their kindergarten days, let anyone tease either of them and he'd have them both to cope with. The solid front they presented against trouble from outsiders was a warm and heartening thing. Always Marcy had looked up to Ken a little, always he had seemed to feel a protective urge toward her.

And it was still that way between them, really. Nothing had changed. Down in her heart, Marcy knew Ken didn't meant to be cruel, anymore than she meant to be snappish and touchy with him. Maybe the friction that seemed to have developed between them lately was just a part of growing up, of not being children anymore. The thought made Marcy feel a little sad.

She looked at Ken and felt his glance deep on hers. Ken—why, he looked as if he had been thinking along exactly the same lines she had, remembering all the times they had stood together, the close bond between them.

Marcy felt a not too willing smile twist her lips as Ken grinned at her.

"Truce?" Ken said.

And Marcy echoed, "Truce." But she couldn't help adding, "I think you're an awful pain sometimes, though."

"You're not too easy to live with yourself these days," Ken told her. "Grow up, why don't you?"

Now that was a funny thing for him to say, Marcy thought. And in such a serious tone, too.

Daddy, who had a regrettably one-track mind in some respects, said, "I still think it was unreasonable of you to ask Mother for a dress like that if you don't intend to wear it."

"But she does intend to, dear," Mom said. "The very first suitable occasion that comes up."

She smiled at Marcy. And Daddy went back to his paper once more, apparently satisfied. And Ken reached out a long arm and turned on some dance music on the radio.

WAIT FOR MARCY

Marcy felt a sick sort of sensation in her tummy. The very first suitable occasion. A dance in the big gym at High, with paper festoons and the lights softened and all the couples, all the girls and their dates, whirling and swaying to just the sort of music that was coming from the radio now. Her lovely white formal would fit into the picture perfectly. But before she could wear it, before she could be a part of the entrancing scene in her mind, someone—who, she wondered a little desperately?—would have to invite her to go with him.

Grow up, why don't you? That was what Ken had said just now. Marcy was trying, but in some respects it wasn't easy. . . .

Chapter Two

THE SUITABLE OCCASION

Lila Rhodes had been a trained nurse before her marriage and as a result everyone in the neighborhood seemed to consider her an expert on minor ailments or injuries. Just let someone feel a slight pain, or let someone's child fall down and cut his knee or bump his head hard enough to raise a lump, and Lila was immediately called in to administer first aid. Often the youthful victims of accident were brought weeping to her door.

"Our front walk," her husband once complained, "has been bled on so often, I feel I could qualify as an expert in removing the gory traces from the scene of any crime."

This particular afternoon it had been Mrs. Miller down the block and one of her dizzy spells that broke into Lila's schedule. She had spent almost an hour at the Millers', waiting till Dr. Carlson's prescription took effect. And now, just as she let herself into her own house once more, the phone began ringing.

"Oh, dear," thought Lila, hurrying to answer it, "if this is another emergency—" She smiled a little at the thought since "Mom's emergencies" had got to be a sort of family joke.

But when she had picked up the phone and said, "Hello?" rather breathlessly for all her rushing, it was a young feminine voice asking for Ken that reached her relieved ears.

"I'm sorry," Lila said. "He isn't here. He said something about playing ping-pong at the Park House with Steve Judson after school."

There was silence, heavy with disappointment, for a moment along the wire. Then, in a slightly embarrassed rush, "This is Karen Blake, Mrs. Rhodes. I wonder if you could tell me something?"

"I'll try," Lila assured her.

"Do you happen to know whether anyone's invited Ken yet to the G.A.A. dance?"

Lila frowned, momentarily puzzled. "Invited Ken?"

"Yes, it's the dance where the girls ask the boys, you know?" A little whisper of a giggle tickled Lila's ear.

Lila remembered about that particular dance then. It was given each year at high school. She had to answer Karen, regretfully, "I'm sorry. I really haven't heard Ken say anything about it so far."

"Gee, haven't you, Mrs. Rhodes? Maybe that means he's still free."

"I don't know," Lila told her. "But I'll have him call you as soon as he comes in."

"Will you? Thanks!"

Lila hung up and stood regarding the phone tentatively for a moment. Then the thought of the lateness of the hour and the time she had spent with Mrs. Miller nudged at her. She hung her jacket in the closet and went out to the kitchen to start dinner. Late afternoon sunlight spilled through the west windows. The row of ivy plants in bright red pots cast little pointed shadows downward from the window sill. But Lila wasn't thinking about her cheerful red-and-white kitchen, or even of the meal she was about to cook. Her hands went with the familiarity of long practice about their necessary tasks. But her mind was engaged almost exclusively with thoughts of the Girls' Athletic Association dance, to which the girls invited the boys. It seemed to her that this might be a heaven-sent opportunity for Marcy's lovely white dress to be given a proper workout. Surely, among her wide circle of schoolmates and friends, there must be some boy Marcy would like to invite. If only she weren't too shy to take the initiative, to make that first difficult step.

Somehow, Lila found herself remembering when she had first learned how to dive. It was one thing to know how—it was another to stand away up there on the diving-board above the water and jump off. She could still recall —good Heavens, it must have been thirty years ago!—how she had stood and shivered, looking down into the limpid blue waters of the pool, afraid to plunge, equally afraid to face the unmerciful teasing of her friends should she stumble back along the diving-board to safety. In the end she had decided a broken neck was definitely the lesser of two evils. And she had dived. She could still remember how proud she had felt—and how easy it had been after that terrifying initial plunge was taken.

Maybe jumping into the social whirl was something like that. Maybe all Marcy needed was a bit of encouragement, a little push. If that were so, certainly her mother should do what she could to help her. . . .

When Marcy got home from school—she had stayed for a while after classes were over to attend an Art Club meeting—there was a marvelous odor of chocolate cupcakes in the air. She put down her books, shrugged out of her scarlet corduroy jacket, and followed her delighted nose out to the kitchen.

"Hi, Mom. You save the cake dough for me?"

There was a standing arrangement between her and Ken

that the first one home, when a cake had been baked, got to scrape out the delicious leavings in the mixing bowl.

"Right there," Lila indicated the bowl on the cabinet.

Marcy got a spoon out of the silverware drawer and fell to. "Ummmm—it's lish. Why didn't you leave more?"

"I needed some of it for cupcakes," Mom said drily. "You like those, too, remember?"

Marcy nodded, smiling. She scraped the last smidgin out of the bowl and set it in the sink, let water run into it.

"How was school?" Mom asked.

"Oh, foul, as usual," Marcy said. She didn't really mind school as much as her tone implied. But it was the sort of thing she would never have admitted. She laughed a little, remembering. "Bix Meyers said the most perfectly screaming thing in History. Laidlaw gave us this gruesome assignment, we have to interpret the meaning of one of George Washington's speeches. And Bix said, right out loud in class, 'Interpret it? I can't even translate it!' Wasn't that a howl?"

Lila had to laugh with Marcy, although she had been listening with only half an ear. Marcy proceeded to help herself to a slice of bread, which she then spread liberally with peanut-butter and jelly. Her mother had long since realized that this practice, common to both her children whenever they got home from school, would have no effect whatever on their subsequent appetite for dinner. And so she offered no objection. In fact, she scarcely noticed what Marcy was doing, so intent was she on her own train of thought.

"Marcy—" Mom's tone sounded tentative.

"Hmmmm?"

"A girl called a little while ago to ask Ken to the G.A.A. dance."

"Who?" Marcy asked, with interest.

"Karen Blake."

Marcy shook her head and spoke thickly through a mouthful of bread and peanut-butter and jelly. "Not a chance. Rosemary's already got him sewed up—not that I can see he's such a prize."

It occurred to Marcy that her mother was regarding her in a very odd way. She would have been much more appalled if she could have fathomed her mother's thoughts. For they were something like this: It simply doesn't make sense for Marcy never to have had a real date. She's as pretty as most of the girls around Westfield. She has loads of friends, boys and girls. Ken's pals are always nice to her when they come to the house, or at least as nice as they'll condescend to be to any of the girls. They clown around with her and tease her. And Marcy argues with them and they rough-house like a bunch of overgrown puppies and the insults fly thick and fast. Why is it, then, that they don't ask Marcy to the dances at school, instead of the Karens and the Rosemarys and pretty little creampuffs like her friend Liz? And, by the same token, why doesn't Marcy ask one of them to this particular dance?

"Marcy," Mom said in a very portentous tone, "who are you planning to invite to the dance?"

Marcy stared at her, chewing automatically, feeling her throat tighten in the way she hated. She tried to make her voice extremely casual, after she had swallowed and was able to get out any words at all. "Oh, I don't think I'll bother with it."

"Why not?" Mom asked, in a definitely pinning-down tone.

"Oh, the G.A. things aren't so sharp."

Mom asked, "How do you know when you haven't gone to any of their dances?" She hurried on then firmly, before Marcy could figure out an answer, "Honey, I think you're making a mistake. I think you should plan on going."

Marcy wet her lips. She said faintly, "It's so dumb—having to ask a boy to take you."

"But two girls have had the courage to invite Ken."

"That's different," Marcy said quickly. "Entirely different."

"Why?"

"Well—" Marcy pushed the toe of one moccasin back and forth on the linoleum floor with a little squeaking sound, "Ken's taken both of them out before. He's taken Rosemary out several times and Karen at least twice."

"I can't see that makes so much difference," Mom argued. She didn't sound quite so positive as she had before, though.

"Oh, but it does, Mom, it does!" Marcy informed her. "You just don't understand."

A kind of pitying look crept into Mom's eyes. She said slowly, "I understand better than you think, dear. After all, I was young once, too. And I can remember—oh, lots of things that probably haven't changed so much as you'd imagine." She went on, "I'm only trying to help you, dear. I can see why you might feel a little shy, but—"

"Shy!" Marcy burst out, appalled. "What a foul word! I'm not shy! I'm not shy the tiniest bit! It's just—just—" her voice died away in the most embarrassing manner. Then she forced out defiantly, "There simply isn't anyone I'd care to invite."

"Even in order to wear your lovely dress?" Mom asked gently.

Marcy shook her head. "It wouldn't be any fun to wear it if I wasn't going someplace I wanted to go, with someone I wanted to go with. All the boys I know—"

Mom asked then, apparently following some train of thought of her own, "How about Steve?"

"Steve!" Marcy stared at her mother, breathing the name as though its single syllable were abhorrent to her. "You—you don't mean Steve Judson?"

"Do we know any other Steves?"

"No—but surely you don't imagine—"

"Why not?" Mom inquired mildly. "He's a very nice boy and your brother's friend. He's good-looking. And so far his mother's been able to restrain him from getting a crew-cut. He—"

"No!" Marcy said positively. "Oh, no!"

"Why not?" Mom asked again. "He's even sort of taken you out. That is, you've gone to the movies a few times with him and Ken. And you've played ping-pong doubles with him and Rosemary and Ken."

"That character!" Marcy spoke scathingly. She turned on her heel and stalked from the room as though she had reached the limit of her endurance, as, indeed, she had. She flung back over her shoulder, "I wouldn't go to a dance with him if he were the last man on earth!"

It might not be an original thing to say, she realized as she ran up the stairs, but it expressed her feelings. Steve Judson—why, he and Ken had been friends since they were in grade school. Imagine going to a dance with a boy you could distinctly remember in short pants! And as for his being good-looking—what a perfectly ridiculous thing for Mom to say! Oh, he was tall enough and his shoulders were quite broad and there wasn't anything actually repulsive about his features. He had dark hair and gray eyes and a rather nice grin, even when he was teasing a girl unmercifully, as he usually was. He called Marcy "Squirt" and "Revolting" just as Ken did, sometimes even

"Dream-puss," although she thought she had finally made it clear that she wouldn't take that from either of them. And he acted as though she were about twelve years old. If Mom imagined for a minute she'd degrade herself so far as to ask Steve Judson to take her anywhere, let alone the G.A. dance, she was just crazy, that was all. A girl, it seemed to Marcy, should be entitled to more understanding from her own mother. Couldn't Mom see how utterly impossible her suggestion was?

To Marcy's complete disgust, hot tears pressed against her eyelids, spilled over. She felt dreadful, all stirred up inside, choking with utter misery. Why couldn't people let her alone, stop trying to make her do things she didn't want to do? She reached the upper hall just in time, yanked open the door of her own room, her sanctuary, and hurrying inside, slammed the door resoundingly after her and flung herself face downward across the bed.

Chapter Three

MARCY OVERHEARS A SECRET

Only a moment after the sound of Marcy's slammed door assaulted her mother's ears, Lila was startled to see Ken amble into the kitchen.

"Well, hello," she said. "I didn't hear you come in."

"Hi, Mom." Ken dropped his ping-pong paddle onto the cabinet with a clatter. His blue eyes were bright with curiosity. "Who could hear anything with that whirlwind going through the house? What's she playing the big scene for, tearing upstairs and slamming her door like a soap-opera heroine?"

Lila had to smile. "Well, I guess I'm to blame, although all I did was make what seemed to me like a good suggestion."

"Oh-oh!" Ken said. "What kind of suggestion?"

"Simply that she consider asking Steve to take her to

the dance that's coming up at school." Lila sighed, turning back to her dinner preparation. "I certainly didn't mean to upset her so."

"She upsets awful easy these days," Ken said, helping himself to an apple from the bowl on the table. "Matter of fact, she could do a whole lot worse than ask ol' Steve."

Suddenly Lila remembered. "Oh—Karen phoned you. I said you'd call her back."

Ken shook his head. "No need to. She tracked me down at the Park House. When I told her I was already dated, she asked Steve."

"And—" Lila inquired with interest.

"He told her 'no soap,' too."

"You mean someone else had already invited him?" Lila knew it was absurd to feel a thrust of disappointment.

Ken bit into his apple with audible relish. "Well, no, not actually, although that was the impression he tried to give Karen. The thing is, he just didn't want to go with her. She's kind of a dim bulb," Ken confided.

Lila swung around from the sink to face him, her glance thoughtful. After a moment she asked, "Just between the two of us, Ken, would you say your sister is a dim bulb, whatever that is exactly?"

Ken appeared to consider the matter, a frown of concentration between his stubby brows. "Well—no," he said judiciously. "It's kind of a funny thing about Marcy. She could be away up there on the Hit Parade with the guys, if only—"

"If only what?" Lila demanded as he stopped.

"Well—that's just it. I don't know exactly what the trouble is. I kind of suspect, but I'm not sure."

Lila suspected, too. She wondered whether Ken's conclusions on the delicate subject of his sister's lack of attention from the boys matched her own. Marcy would be furious if she knew they were discussing her, her mother realized. And yet the knowledge that Ken had been putting some thought on Marcy's problems made Lila feel a little glow of warmth and gratification. All through their childhood, Marcy and Ken had been important to each other, any outside influence affecting either of them had been of vital concern to them both. Now their mother was pleased to know that despite the arguments and squabbles of their teens, the basic closeness between them hadn't changed.

She asked, "Do you think it's something about Marcy's attitude toward the boys?"

Ken nodded. "Yeah, I think that's it. Her looks are okay. She's got all the stuff—only—she doesn't seem to know how to use it. She kind of puts the fellas off some way. Take ol' Steve. He likes Marcy, but does she ever give him a tumble? Still, he hasn't given up hope entirely."

"How do you mean?" his mother asked.

"Well," Ken confided, "that's the reason he turned Karen down. He still figures maybe there's a chance Marcy'll ask him to the dance and he wants to stay free so he can go with her if she does. But you saw the way she acted when you suggested—" Ken broke off abruptly as Marcy appeared in the kitchen doorway, her dark eyes narrowed irately and her hands clenched on her hips. "What's the idea, sneaking up on people like that?" he demanded indignantly.

"I didn't sneak!" Marcy denied hotly. "Anyway, you've got a lot of nerve standing there talking about me—about things that aren't any of your business!"

"You got something there," Ken said drily. "A person ought to be able to figure out a more intelligent subject of conversation."

He tossed his apple core into the waste basket and ambled from the room, hands in pockets, whistling. Marcy glared at him as he passed. He could be heard taking the stairs two at a time, loping down the upper hall. Then his radio blared from his room.

Lila spoke apologetically. "I'm sorry, dear. We weren't discussing you in any—any unkind manner." She could see that Marcy's eyes were suspiciously pink. She hoped she wasn't going to cry again.

"It's okay," Marcy told her in a slightly martyred tone. "I suppose it's too much to expect that a person's private affairs be treated as private. In this house a goldfish ought to feel right at home."

She strolled over to the kitchen stool and sat on it, elbow on knee, chin on palm, reflectively. She wasn't, really, very angry. A kind of lively curiosity crowded resentment almost entirely out of her mind. She recalled Ken's words so clearly. "He still figures maybe there's a chance Marcy'll ask him to the dance and he wants to stay free so he can go with her if she does." Those were Ken's very words and he had spoken them before he had any idea she was within hearing distance. So it must be true —but how could Ken know, Marcy wondered. Unless Steve had told him so. . . . Was it possible that boys talked things like that over, just as girls did? Somehow, she had always supposed that boys' conversation between themselves ran mostly to basket-ball and foot-ball and ping-pong—and movies, maybe—anyway, sort of impersonal things. The thought of Steve Judson and Ken talking about girls—about her!—made her feel queer and uncertain. What else had Steve said about her, she wondered. Ken wouldn't tell her, the stinker. She would never have found out as much as this if he hadn't been talking confidentially to Mom and she hadn't just happened to overhear him. Not that she'd been eavesdropping. She wouldn't do a thing like that. But when a person comes downstairs in her own house and hears her name being mentioned over and over, well, naturally she pricks up her ears.

"Marcy!" She became dimly aware of Mom's somewhat impatient voice addressing her.

"Huh?"

"I've asked you three times not to sulk because your

brother and I were talking about you. If we didn't have your best interests at heart—"

"Who's sulking?" Marcy asked in surprise.

Mom stared at her. "Well, naturally I thought you must be, just sitting there and not answering me."

"I didn't hear you say anything," Marcy informed her. "I was thinking."

Mom shook her head and went back to paring potatoes.

Marcy jumped off the stool. "I'll set the table. And then I've simply got to call up Liz."

She proceeded to set the table fast. Hearing the staccato clink of china and cutlery from the dining-room, Lila cringed a little for the fate of her dishes. But nothing broke. Then Marcy went out into the hallway and picking the phone from its cradle gave the Kendall number.

Liz's voice answered and Marcy said simply, "Me."

"Oh," Liz said. "Wait till I get comfy."

"Umm," Marcy agreed, stretching out on the floor and putting her feet on the telephone bench. This was her favorite position for talking on the phone, especially with Liz. No doubt Liz was getting into much the same position at her end of the wire. They always had so much to talk about and today was no exception, even though they had walked home from school together only half an hour before.

Marcy began, "Liz, the loopiest thing happened."

"What?" her friend demanded.

"My mother," Marcy said pityingly, "suggested that I ask Steve Judson to the G.A. dance."

"Oh, no!" Liz said.

"Yes," Marcy informed her. "That character! Can you imagine?"

Liz couldn't. "Not that he's impossible," she added judiciously, "but you've always found him so annoying."

"That's just it," Marcy agreed. "That's what makes Mom's suggestion so absolutely ridic!"

"Besides," Liz reminded her, "you said you weren't figuring on going at all."

"I'm not," Marcy assured her. "It was just a quaint notion of my mother's."

"Still," Liz said in a thoughtful sort of tone, "maybe you should change your mind and ask someone, Marce. I had kind of a tough time screwing my courage up to the point of asking Bill Weaver. But once I'd done it and he said he'd love to—well, it was sort of like after you get through with a dental appointment—you know, that relieved feeling?"

"It's not a question of courage," Marcy said firmly, "not on my part, anyway. It's just—"

"He's actually kind of cute, if you care for the tall, dark and don't-give-a-darn type," Liz said. "Only thing is, somebody's probably already snagged him for the dance by this time."

"No," Marcy said in her most casual tone. "My brother

says Steve's still free. Karen asked him this afternoon when Ken couldn't go with her, but Steve side-stepped her."

"Hmmm," Liz said thoughtfully. And then, after a moment, "Maybe it's not such a loopy idea on your mother's part at that."

"Oh, Liz!" Marcy rebuked her. "Don't be silly. I wouldn't dream of asking him. Why, he's never taken me out, not on a regular date, that is."

"Still," Liz said, "a girl has to take a little teeny bit of the initiative sometimes. Maybe he's bashful."

Marcy hooted derisively. "That character, bashful? You just haven't seen as much of him as I have, or you wouldn't say a thing like that."

A slight note of envy crept into Liz's tone. "Gee, you're lucky having a brother. With all his friends at your disposal, running in and out of your house all the time, seems to me you'd have more dates than you know what to do with."

"His friends," Marcy informed her, "aren't always the type I like. And anyway, they've been running in and out of our house for years, so most of them don't seem to be able to grasp the fact that I'm grown up now and no longer a mere child. Especially Steve Judson. He's one of the very worst."

And yet, Marcy remembered with a warm little glow, Steve was hoping she'd ask him to the dance. That was what Ken had said and he was certainly in a position to know. She considered passing this juicy bit of additional information along to Liz, then decided against it. There was a quality of excitement in the secret knowledge. To share it, even with her best friend, would dissipate a little of its magic. Marcy lay prone on the floor, talking with Liz, for some time longer. Then the sound of her father's footsteps on the front walk made her terminate the conversation hastily and scramble to her feet. Her telephone conversations with Liz were a rather sore point with her father just now. A few afternoons ago he had tried for a solid hour, at five minute intervals, to call her mother from his office and tell her he wouldn't be able to get home for dinner. But Marcy had been talking to Liz. . . . Parents, she thought, could make such an issue of things, perfectly trivial things, too. . . .

It was the following evening after dinner that Ken asked Marcy casually, "Want to go to the movies, Squirt?"

"With you?"

"Steve and me."

Marcy stared at him. "To whom do I owe the honor of this unexpected invitation?"

"Not to me," Ken said dourly. "Steve's getting soft in the head, I think."

"Oh, you do, do you?" Marcy glared at him. "Well, you can just tell your friend Steve that if he wants to take me to the movies, he can do his own asking!"

"Okay," Ken shrugged, "stay home and do your homework. See if I care, or Steve, either."

Marcy flounced off upstairs, if one can be said to flounce adequately in blue jeans and tee-shirt. She *would* stay home and do her homework and it would be more interesting than going anywhere with those two.

But in her own room, with her books spread on her desk and the lamp adjusted, Marcy found she didn't feel in the mood for studying, after all. The spring night came, softly insistent, through the window. The fragrance of flowering currant, Ken slamming the front door and rushing off to meet Steve in time for the first show, these smells and sounds came up and joined Marcy uninvited. She found herself wondering a trifle wistfully what picture was playing. Not that it mattered, not that she'd have considered going, whatever it was. Steve and his second-hand invitations—who did he think he was, Miles Standish, or somebody?

She considered calling Liz up, or, better still, going over to see her. But then she remembered that Liz wasn't available, she was baby-sitting tonight with the Ericson children. On the heels of this realization, another thought, even more shattering, smote Marcy. This was Friday night! She had forgotten that completely. She didn't have to do her homework yet, there was the whole week-end ahead. She shut her books disgustedly, snapped off her desk light, and went back downstairs. Maybe Mom and

Dad were thinking of going to the movies. If so, she'd go along. And if they ran into Ken and Steve, they could see that she'd even rather go out with her parents than with them. It should prove very shattering to their male egos, especially to Steve's.

But when she reached the living-room, Mom was setting up the card table.

"Oh," Marcy said, "you're playing bridge tonight."

Mom nodded. "We asked the Kendalls over for a few rubbers."

"Oh, well," Marcy sighed.

"Why?" Mom inquired. "Did you want us to do something?"

"No," Marcy shook her head. "Oh, no. I guess I'll go on back upstairs and play some records."

And that was exactly what she did. Only, for some mysterious reason, instead of a loud selection of Spike Jones and Louis Prima, Marcy found that her taste seemed to run to the softer, more romantic type of music, the kind she usually dismissed as corny. Now that was a funny thing. . . .

Chapter Four

BROTHERS ARE SO ANNOYING

On Saturdays Ken worked at the Main Street Market, augmenting his allowance which never seemed quite sufficient for his needs. It wasn't that his allowance was too small, it was more that money seemed to slip through Ken's fingers. His job consisted of helping keep the shelves stocked, assisting customers with heavy bags of groceries out to their cars and, in general, making himself useful around the big, clean store where half of Westfield's housewives did their marketing.

"Good training for him," George Rhodes said. "Maybe he'll learn money doesn't grow on trees, if he has to do something to earn it."

Lila was inclined to agree. Ken was pretty casual about money, still she thought he'd outgrow his tendency to spend freely at the beginning of the week, when he'd just got his allowance, and then have to borrow ahead to last through. At least, his Saturday job wasn't hard enough to hurt him any. He'd had it now for a year.

So it seemed rather strange that Steve Judson, who knew Ken so well, should have forgotten that he wasn't around home on Saturdays. But Steve stopped by at two, ping-pong paddle in hand, his dark hair wet-brushed, but rebellious, his strong-jawed young face looking newly scrubbed and anticipatory. Lila was sitting in the living-room, knitting, so she couldn't help hearing the entire conversation that ensued when Marcy answered his ring at the door-bell.

"Hi, Marce," he said, coming in as Marcy opened the door. "Ken around?"

"Nope, dope. Working, remember?"

Steve snapped his fingers in profound self-disgust. "Golly, I forgot all about that. Just when I felt like a good game, too." He hefted his paddle lovingly. Just then his gray glance edged past Marcy and fell on Lila across the room. "Oh, hello, Mrs. Rhodes," he said pleasantly. "How are you?"

"Fine," Lila smiled. "Won't you sit down, Steve?"

"Well—" his large feet in their shapeless loafers remained planted firmly—"I don't think so. Guess I'll scram on over to the Park House. Maybe there'll be somebody around there I can play with." He shook his head, frowning. " 'Fraid not, though, on a Saturday afternoon."

"Would it kill you," Marcy asked casually, "if you didn't get to play one day?"

A delicious feeling of power swelled in her, a surge of confidence such as she had never felt before. She was positive—well, practically positive—that Steve was just pretending he'd forgotten about Ken being at work. She was almost sure that he had simply used Ken as an excuse for stopping in, that he was carefully maneuvering the situation to the point where he could ask her to play ping-pong with him—and still make it seem as if he hadn't deliberately sought her out. It was a sort of game, Marcy realized, in which one could participate or not, as one chose. There were certain moves to be made, certain others to be avoided. A curious warm sense of excitement made her heart beat a little faster.

"Well—" Steve's gray glance was belligerent and so was the set of his jaw, "I got to keep in practice, I guess."

"What for?" Marcy asked airily.

"There's the tournament next month. I may enter that."

"Hah!" Marcy laughed brutally. "As if you had a chance."

Something inside her, some core older, more experienced, than she had known was there, seemed to have the situation easily in hand. Marcy felt she could afford to relax and let this instinct guide her, indicate just what she should say.

"Is that so?" Steve demanded, scowling down at her.

She hadn't realized before quite how tall he was. "You're a fine one to talk about my chances! I'll bet your game stinks!"

Over on the davenport, Lila sat, frowning just a little, her knitting needles' swift movement momentarily suspended. She didn't know whether to say anything or not. Had the argument been between Marcy and Ken, she would have tried to stop it. But, after all, only one of these belligerents belonged to her. She tried to catch Marcy's eye with a deterring glance. But Marcy wasn't looking at her.

Marcy's shoulder lifted in a casual little shrug. "I could beat you, I'll bet."

Steve snorted. "That I would like to see!" he informed her. "You beating me! That's a laugh, that is."

"I don't see why," Marcy told him. "Ken taught me and he can beat you."

"Not very often, he can't," Steve denied. "Not much more than half the time." Suddenly, Marcy saw his gaze widen, as though at an arresting thought. Only there was something just a little studied about it, not quite spontaneous. "Say," Steve demanded, "what's to stop me taking you on right now? Then we'll see who's so hot! Then we'll find out just how much you got to brag about. Come on, Squirt!"

Their two glances converged on Lila, each questioning.

"Is it okay, Mom," Marcy asked, "if I go over to the

Park House with him for a while?"

"Why—yes," Lila said weakly. . . .

It was almost dinner-time when Marcy got home. She came in, humming, and her father, who was reading the evening paper in his favorite chair, glanced up at her.

"You sound happy," he said.

"Do I?" Marcy went over and gave him a little kiss on his slightly stubbly cheek. "Oooo, you need a shave."

"Shaved this morning," her father said defensively, feeling his chin. "You imagine it."

"Who won, Marcy?" her mother called from the dining-room, where she was starting to set the table.

"Oh, Steve did," Marcy admitted, strolling out to join her. "Here, Mom, I'll do that."

She took the silverware from her mother and began putting it down at each place.

"But didn't you think you could beat him? You said—"

"Oh, no," Marcy shook her head, "I didn't really think so. He's quite good. Beat me every game but three. He says my backhand's lousy. He's going to help me work on it."

"He is?" Lila said.

Marcy smiled at her mother and her mother smiled back at her. A current of communication was established between them, without another word being said. Marcy thought her mother looked relieved, as though she'd been a tiny bit worried about something, but wasn't any longer.

"We had Cokes afterward," Marcy said. "We'd have had hamburgers, too, we were both absolutely starved, but Steve was flat."

"I see," Lila nodded. Apparently Ken wasn't the only one who had trouble stretching his allowance. She asked, "You—didn't say anything to him about the dance, did you?"

"Oh, no!" Marcy said positively. "I told you I wouldn't dream of doing that. I explained all about it to you."

Lila opened her mouth to speak, but Marcy forestalled her. She hurried out to the kitchen for the dishes, tossing back over her shoulder, "What's for dinner? It smells good."

"Meat loaf," her mother said resignedly.

"Oh, yum," Marcy said and the mood for confidences was definitely dissipated.

It was a few nights later, on Wednesday, and the Rhodes family was gathered about their dinner table, just finishing dessert, when Marcy announced, "I've got to hurry. Tonight's Club."

All of them knew perfectly well what she meant. Club was Club and needed no further designation. Club consisted of Marcy and seven other girls and met on alternate weeks at the various members' houses. It had been in existence since the founding members were in sixth grade and had survived so many feuds, crises and upheavals of one sort or another that it seemed destined to go on forever.

"Oh," Mom said. "Where are you meeting tonight?"

"At Betty Graves'."

"Why are you meeting—that's a better question," Ken put in, helping himself to a second generous serving of chocolate cake. "What that bunch of frustrated females bother to keep on getting together for—"

"A lot you know about it," Marcy informed him. "We have fun."

"I'll bet," Ken said drily.

His father looked at him reprovingly. "Why do you take that attitude about your sister's activities? Certainly she has a right to belong to a club if she wants to."

"Well, sure," Ken agreed. "But a club should have some reason. They should do something."

"We do," Marcy snapped. "We do lots of things!"

"What, for instance?"

"Well, we—we talk—and have refreshments—"

"Very constructive," Ken said.

"Why must they do something constructive?" Mom asked. "Lots of clubs are purely social."

"Anyway," Marcy told him, pushing back her chair, "we're just as constructive as that old club you belong to, the one you won't even tell anyone what the letters stand for."

"You mean B.B.P.A.F.B.U.B.S.?" Ken grinned smugly.

Marcy shook her head, appealing to her parents, "You see what I mean? And he calls our club silly. . . ."

She stopped by for Liz Kendall on her way to Club and as they strolled down the street together, with the fragrance of mock orange sweet in their nostrils and the soft spring moonlight filtering through the tree branches overhead, Marcy said, "Brothers are a great trial, Liz. Just be thankful you haven't got any."

Liz sniffed. "Who you kidding?"

"I'm not," Marcy informed her. "Oh, I'll admit I'm fond of Ken, but—"

"You two," Liz said, holding up two fingers pressed close together, "are just like that. You know it and so does Ken! You're thicker than thieves, really. Sometimes I think all this scrapping and squabbling between you is nothing but a pose. Actually either one of you would do anything in the world for the other."

"Well, yes," Marcy agreed thoughtfully, "I suppose that's true enough, if one of us was in a real jam that is. But Ken can be *so* annoying. Of course, he can be very sweet, too—but that comes harder for him."

"What's he done now?" Liz asked.

Marcy proceeded to tell her how Ken had poked fun at the Club at dinner, how he had belittled and ridiculed them, calling them "frustrated females" and implying that their meetings were just a waste of time.

Liz giggled. "It's none of his business, of course, but I can see his point. We don't seem to accomplish a lot except a good deal of gab."

"Neither does his club," Marcy insisted. "He hasn't any right to make remarks about us. That silly string of letters he belongs to."

"What are they again?" Liz asked.

Marcy thought a moment. "B.B.P.A.F.B.U.B.S.—I think."

"I suppose the final 's' stands for Society, don't you?"

Marcy nodded. "I suppose so."

The rest of their walk to Betty Graves' house was taken up with speculation as to just what the mysterious letters stood for. Some of their guesses were so funny that they arrived at their destination with tears of laughter in their eyes. And nothing would do but they must tell all the rest of the Club members what was so funny. As a result, the conversation at Club meeting that night was devoted almost entirely to the meaning of B.B.P.A.F.B.U.-B.S. No one, however, was able to come up with any very likely solution of the mystery. Finally someone suggested that they ought to get around to reading the minutes of the last meeting. So that was done. Then Betty offered to play some new dance records she had acquired since they had been together. So they listened to those. That was the way the evening went. Everyone was astonished when

Betty's mother called them all out to the dining-room for refreshments. They'd had no idea it was ten o'clock. Where had the time gone?

Just as they were sitting down at the table, the doorbell rang. The sound was so unexpected that the high chatter of young feminine voices was stilled momentarily. And Mrs. Graves went to the front door in a dead silence.

So that everyone heard quite clearly when Ken Rhodes' voice drawled, "D'you mind if we kind of crash Club meeting, Mrs. Graves?"

And Steve Judson added, "We figured there might be somebody here who'd need a body-guard going home. It's dark outside. . . ."

Mom and Dad were still up when Marcy got home. Mom's eyes widened just a little in surprise as Ken trailed his sister in. Certainly they hadn't gone out together.

"Mom, it was awful!" Marcy exclaimed, feeling the hot color flood her cheeks all over again at the mere memory. "Ken and Steve crashed the meeting—I was never so embarrassed in my whole life!"

Lila frowned. It seemed to her there was a definite discrepancy between the shocked outrage of Marcy's tone and the self-satisfied gleam in her eye. Could she imagine it, she wondered. Apparently George seemed not to notice it.

He spoke severely. "Ken, I'm surprised at you—and

Steve, too—bothering the girls like that."

"Aw," Ken objected, "she's exaggerating as usual. We didn't go till the meeting was just about over."

"We were having our refreshments," Marcy said.

"Well, natch," Ken grinned. "What better time? Mrs. Graves didn't care. She had plenty of Cokes and cake and stuff."

"But—you two boys and eight girls?" Mom asked tentatively. "Wasn't that a little lopsided?"

"Yeah," Ken admitted a shade morosely. "But it wasn't my idea."

"That Steve!" Marcy exclaimed, her eyes shining. "That character! I don't know what's got into him. And then, as if I wasn't already humiliated enough, he and Ken insisted on walking Liz and me home!"

"You were the only two out of that bunch of bags we'd be caught dead with," Ken growled. "Anyway, ol' Steve and I were together, so I stuck with him."

Marcy sighed, deeply. "Well, I'm going to bed." Her voice took on a warning note. "And don't you two ever pull another trick like that!"

She stalked from the room indignantly, up the stairs.

Ken grinned feebly at his parents. "Guess I'll hit the sack, too."

George started to speak, but Lila forestalled him adroitly. "I think you'd better, Ken. It's quite late and tomorrow's a school day. Good-night."

Not until Ken was out of hearing did George inquire pointedly of his wife, "Am I to take it you approve of his conduct? I felt Marcy was entirely justified in her objection to being put in an embarrassing position."

Lila nodded thoughtfully. "I think she was justified, too, dear. It's just—I'm not quite sure she was embarrassed."

"But she had every cause to be."

"Did she?" A little smile curved Lila's lips. "I seem to remember when I was fifteen, I wasn't too put out when someone young and male turned up demanding to take me home from a party. Even if he was accompanied by my brother."

George grinned, too. "Well, you should know more about the feelings of a fifteen-year-old female than I. But I don't like to let Ken get away with too much."

"Neither do I," Lila agreed. "But—well, I just have a hunch we shouldn't be too severe with him about this. I have a funny feeling that there's something a little bit odd going on, something that hasn't come out into the open yet."

Her husband sighed. "Kids!" he said resignedly. . . .

Chapter Five

A GIRL CAN CHANGE HER MIND

On several occasions during the following week, Steve Judson happened to call the house when Ken wasn't home. He seemed to have developed a positive knack for missing him. And each time Marcy happened to answer the telephone.

"I'll take it, Mom," she would yell at the bell's first jingle. And she would come clumping down the stairs from her room, or rush in from the kitchen, or wherever she might be. "I'm expecting a buzz from Liz."

She would breathe a slightly breathless, "Hello?" into the mouthpiece. And then Mom would hear her say, disappointed, "Oh, it's you. . . . No, he's not here. . . . Nope, I haven't the slightest idea. . . . What do you think I am, his social secretary? . . ." And so on and on. And on.

Marcy even got into the habit of lying flat on her back on the floor, her feet propped on the telephone bench, to talk with Steve, just as she did when she talked with Liz. Not that Mom blamed her exactly. Her conversations with Steve were almost as long as with Liz. Sometimes they went on for half an hour, all devoted to heated argument, barbed insults and repeated threats to hang up—threats, however, which didn't quite materialize. And after each conversation, Marcy seemed wrapped in a dreamy mellow mood for some time. She would sit sprawled low on the couch, her ankles crossed far out in front of her, her eyes fixed on space. Or she might go up to her room and play all her most sentimental records. She always closed her bed-room door carefully before she did this, as though a leaning toward "Stardust" and "Smoke Gets In Your Eyes" were somehow shameful.

Still, whenever Steve's name came up in casual family talk, Marcy dismissed him quite as scathingly as before. It was as though, thought Mom, she were being pulled two ways and wasn't certain yet which force she would give in to.

Marcy herself couldn't quite fathom what was happening to her. She felt uncertain of her own reactions. Take the sound of Steve's voice on the phone—once she honestly would have been disappointed it wasn't Liz. Now her heart would beat faster and she would feel a curious swooping sensation in her tummy, like going down too fast in an elevator. And she would be quite incapable of putting a decisive end to their conversation, of telling Steve Ken wasn't home and to call back later. No, she would feel this irresistible urge to talk on and on, this strange reluctance to hang up the receiver and go about her own business.

If only she hadn't overheard Mom and Ken talking in the kitchen that day and learned that Steve actually liked her, that he was hoping she'd ask him to the dance. That was when this strange unrest and uncertainty had begun in her. But if he liked her, wasn't there some way he could indicate it, something he could say, or do? But maybe, Marcy reminded herself, he was trying to indicate his feelings by the loopy way he acted lately. Like dropping in that Saturday to play ping-pong when he knew darned well Ken was at work. And that exhibition he'd talked Ken into making of themselves, crashing Club to bring her and Liz home. Maybe, her breath hurried just a little at the thought, Steve was feeling as mixed-up and uncertain as she, maybe he didn't quite know what to do about it, either.

She supposed it might be a little hard for a boy to come right out and ask for a date with a girl who was the sister of his best friend, a girl he'd got into the habit of teasing and kidding and considering a mere child. But he surely couldn't expect her to make the first move and ask for a date! No, he'd simply have to work it out for himself, Marcy thought, sighing. . . .

Meantime, the date of the dance drew nearer. Marcy wasn't the only one who realized that. Mom was growing more and more anxious. Every time she cleaned Marcy's room, the lovely white net formal seemed to reproach her mutely from its plastic garment-bag prison. Like a princess locked in a cruel enchantment, who needed a prince's kiss to awaken her. Only all the white formal needed was for Marcy to ask Steve to take her to the dance. But that, it seemed, Marcy would not do.

The dance was a mere week off on the Friday evening when Marcy popped into the kitchen just before dinnertime to ask, her young face alight, "Can I help, Mom? Will it be ready soon? We want to make the early show."

"Who?" Mom asked, her spoon poised over the gravy, bubbling rich and brown in the frying pan.

"Steve and I and Liz and Ken—we're double-dating." The last word tasted strange, but sweet, on Marcy's lips. "Steve called up just a few minutes ago. Didn't you hear the phone? Then Ken called Liz and it's all set."

Ken stuck his head over Marcy's shoulder in the kitchen doorway. He said dourly, but with a gleam in his eye Mom couldn't miss, "It wasn't my idea. I can live without Liz Kendall's company. But poor ol' Steve's got this yen for Marcy." He ducked as Marcy swung her open hand at him, then raced off through the house with his sister in close pursuit.

Hearing the sound of their laughter, Lila smiled, too.

She stirred the gravy faster than ever, so that the early show might be made. . . .

Lila and George were in bed that night when their children got home. George was sound asleep, but Lila was awake just enough to observe a rather strange phenomenon. A good half hour elapsed between the time when she heard Ken's heavy step on the stairs and Marcy's considerably lighter tread. And in between the two, Lila was drowsily aware of a vague murmur of voices from the porch below. Voices that droned on and on, breaking now and then into the muffled sound of laughter. But surely Marcy wouldn't stand talking all that time to Steve Judson! As soon as she heard her daughter come in and go to her room, Lila fell asleep without having thought the puzzling matter entirely through. But looking back the next morning, she wondered.

She wondered so much that she went into Marcy's room around eight o'clock to see if she was awake yet. Rather surprisingly on a Saturday, Marcy was not only awake, but up. She was not only up, but dressed. She was not only dressed, but wearing her white net formal, posing in it, in fact, before the full-length mirror on her closet door.

The glass gave back her young reflection sweetly. The dress was still long enough, Mom saw with a sense of relief. And Marcy looked lovely in it. Mom thought, a little catch in her throat, "When she has some satin slippers, instead of those awful loafers she's wearing—and flowers in her hair—"

She asked gently, "You're thinking of wearing it somewhere?"

Marcy whirled around and the full skirt billowed. She spoke and although her voice was casual in the extreme, excitement made her eyes sparkle and dance and a little smile curved her mouth. "Oh, yes," she said, "I'm planning to. So long as it means so much to you and Daddy, I decided I would go to the dance after all. Then you won't feel I'm wasting Gran's gift."

"Well, good," Mom said. "I'm glad, dear."

Their eyes met and a little current of wordless communication ran between them, strong and sure. Mom knew Marcy's casual attitude was just a pose and Marcy knew she knew. Marcy didn't care, actually. It was fun to pose a little, to assume a woman-of-the-world attitude, at fifteen.

"Steve's taking me," Marcy said airily. "I'll probably have a horrible time. But—he's just been hanging around so much lately, I could hardly avoid asking him. I mean I felt he sort of expected it. And I wouldn't exactly want to hurt his feelings, when he and Ken are such good friends."

"Well, no," Mom agreed gravely. "It would be a shame to hurt his feelings. He's a nice boy."

"He's okay," Marcy said, turning back to the mirror

once more, "when you get to know him. Anyway, I asked him last night. And it's all set. He's even practically sure his father'll let him take their car."

"That'll be fine," Mom said, "just fine."

She left Marcy then and went on down the hallway to Ken's room. Once inside she shut the door quietly behind her. It wasn't so surprising to find Ken up. He was due at the Main Street Market at nine. But he was still in his pajama pants—the top half of any pair of pajamas was a total loss so far as Ken was concerned—and his blond head was tousled. He was sitting at his desk with a piece of paper before him, a stub of pencil gripped in his fingers.

"Ken," Mom said, "it worked. She asked him."

Ken grinned up at her. "Saw through me all the time, didn't you? Kinda foxy."

Mom shook her head. "Not foxy. Not even too bright, or I'd have seen from the start what you were maneuvering toward."

"Didn't you?"

"No, I was just vaguely aware of wires being unobtrusively pulled in the background."

Ken grinned. "Me and that Italian we read about in Ancient History. What was his name—Machiavelli, or something?"

"Just what did you do exactly?" Mom wanted to know.

"Oh, nothing much," Ken said modestly. "Remember

that day you and I were talking about Marcy and the dance and stuff and you said you had suggested she ask Steve and she got so mad?"

"Yes, of course. And she came down and heard us—"

"I heard her coming," Ken confided, "so I gave you all that line about Steve thinking she was so swell and wishing she'd ask him to the dance."

"Line?" Mom stared at him blankly. "But—you said he turned down Karen's invitation."

Ken shrugged. "Who wouldn't?"

"You mean," Mom asked faintly, "it wasn't true about him liking Marcy?"

Again Ken's bare tanned shoulders moved up and down. "I don't know. If it was, Steve hadn't got around to mentioning it to me. But anybody knows a girl will get interested in a guy every time if she thinks he's carrying a secret torch for her. It's elemental."

"Oh," Mom said. "And—was that all you did?"

"Well—" Ken grinned, "it works both ways, you know. So I kind of dropped a couple of hints to ol' Steve that Marcy thought he was pretty terrific. I didn't do much," he assured Mom earnestly. "It was just a question of getting them thinking about each other."

"So it was just a question of that." Mom's glance fell on the paper on his desk. Her brows rose in surprise. "Writing poetry, Ken?"

"Aw, no," he disclaimed, embarrassed. "It's just something to go with the corsage I'm getting Rosemary for the dance." His nod gave her permission to look closer. Mom leaned down and read:

"Roses are red,
Violets are blue,
Orchids cost five bucks—
Here's carnations for you."

Her eyes lifted to meet Ken's and her smile was gentle. "Question of money?"

Ken nodded. "As usual."

Mom reached out and took the sheet of paper. She tore it once across and then once again and dropped the scraps into the wastebasket. "Orchids it shall be," she said firmly, "at my expense."

"Gee, thanks, Mom. Did I ever tell you you're my favorite woman?"

Sometimes, Mom thought, Cupid wasn't a rosy infant with a quiver full of arrows at all. He could be a lanky seventeen-year-old with a kind heart, an enduring fondness for a kid sister, and an understanding of psychology far beyond his years. Brothers, she reflected as she left Ken to get dressed and went on downstairs to start his breakfast, were a wonderful institution. No girl should be without one.

Chapter Six

THE DANCE

The next week seemed to pass, for Marcy, in an airy dream. Every minute, except the time a ruthless educational system decreed must be spent at school, was filled to the brim with thoughts of Saturday night and the dance. Plans and decisions of an excitingly momentous sort crowded in upon her. What to wear was already settled. But—how to do her hair? Whether it would be best to have it washed and set a day ahead or on Saturday morning for the most satisfactory results? Whether to wear high heels or low? Since she was getting new evening sandals for the occasion, the choice was entirely up to her. Finally she decided on low heels, because Liz liked low heels best and Liz had more experience with dancing slippers than she.

"Isn't it all fun?" Liz exclaimed as she and Marcy

strolled home together after buying Marcy's satin sandals. "Aren't you thrilled?"

"Well—sort of," Marcy admitted, cuddling the shoe box under her elbow. Actually she was so delightfully excited she was having a hard time making her feet touch the ground at each step. "Not over Steve, of course," she informed Liz. "Just the dance and all."

Liz nodded. "Oh, sure. That's why I'm excited, too. But Bill's pretty sharp. I'm glad I asked him."

Marcy merely smiled. She was thinking that, as a matter of hard fact, Steve was quite a bit more attractive than Bill Weaver. He wasn't so tall as Bill, but there was such a thing as being too tall, really. And Steve's shoulders were broader and he had a cuter smile. In fact, all his features were quite satisfactory. And she had always liked that sort of crisp-looking dark hair—

She snapped out of her reverie with a start as Liz demanded, a shade impatiently, "Aren't you?"

"Aren't I—what?" Marcy had to ask.

Liz sighed. "Stick around, why don't you, and listen to what I'm saying? I asked if you weren't glad you'd invited Steve."

"Oh—oh, yes," Marcy said. "Steve's okay. He asked me in Math today what kind of corsage I wanted."

"What did you tell him?"

"Oh, I just said anything that would go with a white

dress—and almost anything goes with white, I guess. I left it up to him."

Liz shook her blond head pityingly. "You'll learn better than that, my dear girl. Maybe his judgment's okay, but some men have the loopiest ideas about what sort of flowers a girl likes."

"They do?" Marcy asked doubtfully.

Liz nodded. "Once a long time ago—you remember last year when I dated Buzz Merrill?—he sent me red roses to go with a pink dress! Can you imagine? Some men are so stupid!"

"Gee!" Marcy exclaimed, appalled at the proportions of this catastrophe. "What did you do, Liz?"

"Do?" Liz moaned. "What could I do? The flowers weren't delivered till late afternoon the day of the dance. All the stores were closed by that time, so I couldn't buy another dress, even if I'd been able to persuade my father to come through with one."

"Didn't you have an old formal you could wear?"

"Too short," Liz confided. "I was still growing revoltingly."

"Well—couldn't you have got another corsage?"

"Buzz would have been mad," Liz explained, "and at that time I still cared. No, there was simply nothing to do, except borrow my mother's taffeta evening skirt—fortunately it's black—and fix up a kind of off-the-shoulder dingus with my nylon peasant blouse. The red roses went fine with that."

Marcy said admiringly, "You're so clever, Liz. I wouldn't have known what to do. I would have simply died."

"Oh, no," Liz said, "you get smartened up to angles like that when you've been going out with boys for a while. Now that you've started dating, you'll get onto things, too."

"Do you really suppose I will?" Marcy asked wonderingly.

"Now that you've started dating"—the phrase echoed pleasantly through her mind. Excitement and anticipation bubbled up in her. Now that the ice had been broken, would this fascinating business of dating go on and on, would she find herself miraculously invited to go places with one boy after another? Would she be popular like Liz? Would Steve take her to the movies, or skating, even to another dance, perhaps, one where he had to do the inviting? And would boys hover around her at picnics, as they hovered around Liz and Rosemary? Marcy hoped so. Her eyes shone at the mere enchanting possibility.

"Hey!" Liz's voice yanked her unceremoniously back to the present. "What are you day-dreaming about now? I asked you what sort of corsage Ken's giving Rosemary."

"I'm sorry," Marcy apologized. "He's getting her an orchid."

"Wow!" Liz exclaimed enviously.

"That's just what I said," Marcy agreed. "I don't see how he can afford it. He's always broke. And I don't think he'd ask Uncle Matt for credit at the flower shop, even if he is a relative. Mom and Dad are always awfully strict about anything like that."

Liz shrugged. "Anyway, Rosemary's a lucky woman. I've only had one orchid in my whole entire life."

"I've never even had one," Marcy admitted wistfully. . . .

Every now and then, during that madly exciting week, the remote possibility that Steve might get her an orchid suggested itself to Marcy. Still, orchids were awfully expensive. And gardenias were just as pretty, really. So were roses and carnations. They weren't quite so unusual, that was all. But she had told Steve to use his own judgment. There was no point in getting herself into a useless tizzy.

She was doing her nails late Saturday afternoon when the door-bell rang and she glanced up to see the Cameron Flower Shop delivery truck parked on the drive. She flew to the door, blowing her fingernails to dry the polish.

"Hi," Willie Barton, her uncle's errand boy and assistant around the green-house, greeted her. His freckled, good-natured face was wreathed in a wider-than-usual grin. He held out a square green box on the tips of his spread fingers. "For a Miss Marcy Rhodes. Anybody by that name live here?"

"Oh, Willie, stop teasing," Marcy admonished him, feeling warm color creep up across her face. "Thanks for bringing this. I'll bet you're busy today."

Willie made a circle with thumb and forefinger as Marcy took the box from him. "Glad to oblige. Dances are great for our business. Always happy to see another girl grow old enough to start gettin' corsages."

He ambled back to the truck, whistling, and Marcy closed the door carefully, so as not to smear her nail polish. She tested it gingerly to be sure it was dry, then, reassured, she devoted her full attention to opening the box containing Steve's flowers.

"Mom," she called across her shoulder, her fingers busy with the string, "it's come—my corsage."

"I'll be right there," Mom called from upstairs. She sounded almost as excited and thrilled as Marcy felt. Her heels thudded quickly down the carpeted stairs.

Together they leaned over the square box as Marcy lifted the lid and folded back the green waxed paper. Color greeted their eyes, a warm rich red, paling just a little toward the edges, contrasting with glossy, dark green leaves.

"Camellias," Mom breathed. "Oh, Marcy, they'll be

simply lovely with your dress."

Marcy's enchanted eyes lifted to Mom's, then returned to the flowers once more. Carefully she took them from their nest of paper. Never had she seen anything more beautiful, more perfect. The thought of Steve selecting them especially for her, to go with her dress and none other, made her heart bump a little.

Aloud she said calmly, "They are nice, aren't they?" She held them against the shoulder of her tee-shirt, felt the cool smooth petals caress her throat. "Never knew Steve had such good taste."

Mom smiled at her. "Fraud!" she said. "You know you're just as thrilled over them as I am."

Marcy smiled, too. But, of course, she wouldn't admit it.

After the flowers had been put away carefully again in their box and carried out to the back porch where it was quite cool, Marcy and Mom sat down on the couch side by side and Marcy went on with her interrupted job of doing her nails.

"Your polish matches the camellias," Mom pointed out.

"So it does," Marcy agreed.

Mom's glance was inquiring. "You're not disappointed, are you? Because Steve didn't send orchids?"

"Orchids?" Marcy repeated in surprise. "I like camellias much better." And it was true, she realized. But not even to herself would she admit that she would have felt the same way about any flowers Steve sent.

Mom smiled. "I hope you have a perfectly wonderful time, dear." Her face sobered. "How do they work it now at dances? Is there a stag line and lots of cutting in, the way there used to be?"

"Oh, no," Marcy told her, "not at school dances. You dance with the boy you go with. And he arranges to swap dances with some of his friends."

Mom nodded. "I think I like that way better. Cutting in used to lead to a lot of hurts and disappointments. If a girl wasn't awfully popular, her partner might get stuck with her, none of the stags would cut in, and she'd be dreadfully embarrassed."

Marcy cringed at the very thought. She, too, liked the present system better. She asked, "Did you get cut in on a lot, Mom?"

A little smile played around her mother's lips, her blue eyes had a faraway, dreamy look. "Often enough," she said. "I'd say I was an average success with the stag line, not one of the top ten, maybe, who never danced more than a couple of feet with the same partner. But, on the other hand, nobody ever got stuck with me long enough to give him any anxious moments. There was one boy—I'll never forget it, I thought it was the most cruel thing I ever saw!—who danced with a five dollar bill in his hand behind a girl's back, meaning he'd pay that much to have her taken off his hands. If she'd known, she'd have cried with embarrassment."

"But how awful!" Marcy said. "Did some stag take him up on it?"

"I think she finally made some excuse and left him, said she wanted to powder her nose, or something of the sort. The powder room was a refuge in those days for unpopular girls."

"But dances can't have been much fun," Marcy objected.

"We enjoyed them," Mom said, "in our barbaric way. But the funny thing is, some of the girls who were the very most popular haven't had nearly as happy lives as those who weren't. Some didn't marry at all and some have been divorced. While some of the girls we used to feel sorry for have wonderful husbands now and nice families and lovely homes."

"Even the one whose mean partner held the five dollar bill?"

Mom nodded. "Even she."

"Who is she now?" Marcy asked. "Do I know her?"

Mom shook her head. "No, she doesn't live in Westfield anymore. She got a job in Chicago when she finished school, then married her boss. The last time she came back on a visit, she was wearing real pearls and a fur coat and had perfectly adorable twin daughters."

"Well, what do you know!" Marcy said.

It was fun, sitting there on the couch, talking woman-to-woman with Mom and realizing that in just a few hours Steve would be calling for her. . . . Marcy's thoughts spun themselves out into such an enticing day-dream that she wasn't even aware of it when Mom got smilingly to her feet and made her way upstairs to finish the job she had been busy with when the arrival of Marcy's corsage interrupted her.

The evening proved nearly as wonderful as Marcy hoped it would be and that was very wonderful indeed. Steve was a breath-taking sight when he called for Marcy in his white dinner jacket and black trousers with the knife-edge crease. Of course, she had had some slight forewarning of his unaccustomed elegance. She had seen how impressive Ken looked in his dinner jacket. As a matter of fact, she had even had to tie his tie for him. Boys were so helpless.

Steve was standing in the living-room, talking to Marcy's father, when she came downstairs. She floated in, her white skirts drifting about her and all the little flecks of silver sparkling like stars. Her hair, over which she had been ready to weep an hour ago, looked soft and natural, its tendency to be too curly entirely tamed. In her hand she carried Steve's camellias.

"Wow!" Steve said and there was a look in his dark eyes Marcy had never seen there before. A dazzled look.

Her father looked just a little dazzled, too, Marcy thought. And Mom, sitting on the couch in the background, was almost purring.

"You look very sweet, dear," Mom said.

Dad frowned just a little, turning toward Mom inquiringly, "You're sure, Lila, that dress isn't too—"

"I'm sure, George," Mom said in a reproving tone.

Steve had regained his equilibrium by that time. He said teasingly, "You really oughta warn a guy when you're going all glamorous on him, so he'd be prepared."

Marcy's smile was inscrutable. "You expected me to wear my blue jeans?"

"Isn't there some happy medium between that and making like a movie starlet on her way to a preview?" Steve asked.

Marcy laughed up at him, feeling all happy and glowing. It was wonderful to hear Steve compare her to a movie star. It was wonderful to be going to the dance with him. Everything was wonderful. Just everything . . .

When they got to the dance, the gym was just as Marcy had thought it would be, the lights softened with crepe paper, the decorations transforming the place from its usual school-day aspect into surroundings strange and enchanting. Everyone looked different, the girls so lovely in their long dresses, the boys so handsome in dinner jackets, their hair slicked back, even their cow-licks subdued for the occasion. It was wonderful and she, Marcy, was a part of it all. For the first time. The very first time.

"Music's not so hot," Steve said, holding her close, but not too close, leading her just right among the dancing couples.

Marcy thought it was wonderful. She was in no mood to be discriminating. But, of course, she didn't say so.

She said, "Well, what do you expect at a G.A. dance?"

"That's right," Steve agreed. "This isn't the Stork Club."

Marcy didn't care. She saw Liz across the crowded floor, dancing with her Bill, she saw Rosemary and Ken, ever so many other familiar faces. She waved and spoke and smiled. Who could want more?

Steve said, and his voice sounded sort of husky, or maybe it was just that Marcy wasn't used to hearing Steve's voice coming from so close, only a couple of inches above her ear, "You're—sure different tonight, Marcy."

"It's just the dress," Marcy said, smiling a little, "and your corsage and all. I'm the same."

"Huh-uh!" Steve denied positively. "You're different, too."

"How different?" Marcy asked.

"Well—uh—for one thing, you're so pretty, Marce."

It was fun to be in the position to do the teasing, rather

than being teased. "You mean I looked so horrible before?"

"No!" Steve said. "No, I don't mean that. You always looked okay. But surely I'd have realized how pretty you were sooner, if it wasn't that you've changed."

Marcy hoped he couldn't feel her heart bumping. She said, "I'm not really pretty. Take Liz now—"

"Liz!" Steve said in vast disdain.

"Look at her," Marcy said, "in that blue dress. Why—"

"I'd rather look at you," Steve told her. "Only I can't get over what's so different about you. You even talk different."

"Do I?" Marcy asked in surprise. "Do I sound—older?"

"Yeah." Steve spoke wonderingly. "Yeah, I guess that is it. You don't sound like Ken's kid sister any more. You sound like—somebody special."

"Then maybe," Marcy said, "you'll stop calling me 'Squirt.' "

"Well, gee, yes," Steve said in a sort of appalled tone. "I never knew you really minded."

The music stopped then and Marcy saw Rosemary and Ken heading their way. Liz and Bill Weaver were moving toward them from the opposite direction. Steve gave her hand a tight squeeze before releasing it. His smile seemed to wrap Marcy up in its admiring warmth, to make her feel cherished and appreciated.

He said, just before the others got within hearing distance, "I wish now I'd been a little stingier swapping dances. You've got two with Bill and one with Ken and one with Bix Meyers. But don't go forgetting who you came with."

A delicious sense of power swelled in Marcy. What had she been afraid of, why had she hesitated? If this was a sample, growing up was going to be fun.

"I won't," she told Steve demurely. . . .

Chapter Seven

VISITING GIRL

By the time school was out in June, Marcy had had several dates with Steve. She had also gone out a few times with Bix Meyers, who was so excruciatingly funny. Bix was good-looking, as well as humorous, and added to his other charms was the fact that he owned a third-or-fourth-hand convertible, which he had paid for with money earned at his last summer's job working as life-guard at the country club pool. But despite Bix's wit, looks and convertible, Marcy still liked Steve best. She guessed there was no accounting for tastes. Not that she let Steve or anyone else know how high he ranked in her estimation. Ken suspected, she knew, but that was only because Ken had always seemed to be pretty well aware of what was going on in her mind.

"Steve's a right guy," Ken told her once in a rarely confidential mood. "But don't go concentrating on him too much just because of that. There are a lot of right guys in the world. Have fun while you're young. That's my motto."

"Ummm," Marcy said thoughtfully. "I think Rosemary'd like it better if you believed in going steady."

"Maybe Rosemary would, but I wouldn't."

"Still you'll be a Senior next year," Marcy reminded him. "And lots of Seniors go steady."

"Let 'em," Ken said. "I still mean to continue in my infantile way, circulating freely." He stared penetratingly at Marcy. "Don't tell me you're thinking of going steady!"

"Oh, no," Marcy disclaimed. "I think I'm too young."

"Well, I'm glad you've got that much sense."

"Besides," she added truthfully, "nobody asked me to."

"Nobody better," Ken said. . . .

With the close of school, a problem arose in the Rhodes household, one that took several stormy sessions to thresh out. Ken was bent and determined to get a full-time summer job. His mother and father strongly opposed the idea. Marcy was neutral.

"I think you should spend more time out-of-doors, get more exercise than you possibly could if you take a job," Mom argued. "Besides, there aren't too many summer jobs to be had. Leave them to the boys who really need the money."

"I need the money," Ken insisted. "I'm always broke. Just working Saturdays isn't near enough to keep me going."

"You also have your allowance," his father pointed out. "And I have no objection to your doing some yard work for some of the neighbors after you've finished ours."

"Yeah, but that's so uncertain," Ken said. "I never know how much I can count on for sure. And I'm already in debt to you. I'm three weeks ahead on my allowance right now."

Marcy felt her heart go out to him in sympathy. Not for worlds would she have divulged that he also owed her three dollars and eighty-five cents, accumulated in little dibs and dabs.

"Yes," Dad said meaningfully, "I know. But you'll have to learn to live within your income. If more people did that, the whole country would be better off. If you can't make ends meet at seventeen, how do you expect to when you're grown up?"

"Yeah, but that's why I want to work this summer—so I can make ends meet."

Mom shook her head. "What about that long bike trip you and Steve were talking about last winter? That would be so good for you. All the fresh air and exercise."

"Oh, crud," Ken said disgustedly. "You make me

sound like an invalid or something who's got to build himself up! I'm strong as a horse and perfectly healthy. And I don't even know if Steve's still figuring on the trip."

"Anyway," Mom said, "a full-time job would be too confining."

The discussion went on and on. And in the end, as parents have a way of doing, Mom and Dad won out. Privately, Marcy didn't think Ken minded as much as he let on. He liked sports and being outdoors a lot as well as the next person. And Steve's family didn't want him working steadily all summer, either, so Ken would have someone to pal around with. Ken did succeed in talking his father into a slight raise in his allowance. Could that have been what he was working toward all along, Marcy wondered. But surely Ken wasn't that subtle.

It didn't take long to settle down into the pleasant lazy routine of vacation. Sleeping late in the morning, helping Mom a bit around the house, then lying outdoors in the sunshine, getting a good tan. Playing tennis and badminton, going on bike hikes and picnics around the lake. Marcy loved it. She wished summer could go on forever. And this was, really, the nicest summer she'd known. Steve was always dropping by, suggesting they go uptown for sodas, or making dates to take her to the movies, or go somewhere with Ken and Rosemary, or Liz and Bill.

VISITING GIRL

And then, in July, it happened. Something, it seemed to Marcy, always had to happen. Things couldn't go on being perfect for very long. Fate wouldn't let them, she guessed.

In this case the instrument Fate wielded was Liz Kendall's cousin, Devon Merriott.

"She's coming for a visit," Liz informed Marcy with a singular lack of enthusiasm. "Next week."

The two girls were lying on a blanket in the Kendalls' back yard, garbed in shorts and halters and armed with sun glasses and a big bottle of sun-tan lotion. They were lying on their tummies at the moment, intent on tanning the backs of their legs, which, with customary perversity, had failed to keep up with the fronts.

Marcy raised herself onto her elbows to regard Liz with interest. "How old is she?"

"Sixteen—almost seventeen, I guess. She's just about a year older than me. I haven't seen her since we were ten or so."

"It sounds like it would be fun to have her stay with you," Marcy said. "Where does she live?"

"New York."

"City?" Marcy asked, her eyes widening.

Liz nodded morosely. She picked a blade of grass and chewed it. She said doubtfully, "Maybe she's improved since I saw her."

"What was wrong with her?" Marcy asked.

"She was an at-bray," Liz said, resorting to pig-Latin as they sometimes did in confidential moments, "of the first water!"

"A real inker-stay?" Marcy asked.

Liz nodded once more. "I couldn't wait for her to go home. I hope it won't be like that this time."

"What did she do?" Marcy asked, intrigued.

Liz shrugged. "Oh, kid stuff—actually I don't remember half of it. I guess it's like we learned in psychology, the way you can build up a wall in your mind and shut off unpleasant things you'd rather forget ever happened."

"That bad?" Marcy's tone was sympathetic. "And she has such a pretty name, too. Devon," she repeated. "I never heard it before. Devon Merriott sounds sort of like a movie star."

"I wish she was," Liz said. "Then she could stay in Hollywood and not have to come to visit here."

"How long will she stay?"

"A month," Liz sighed. "The whole entire month of July. Could she pick a month with only thirty days—no. It has to be thirty-one days. Her mother and father are going to Europe and she's coming here. What a break for the Europeans!"

Marcy said comfortingly, "But she could have improved, Liz. You said so yourself."

Liz moaned. "I always was an optimist. . . ."

It was Mrs. Kendall's idea to give a party the Saturday

night following her niece's arrival. "Just so she can get to know your friends, dear," she explained to Liz, "and feel more at home among you."

Liz was apathetic about it all, but she did invite the crowd over. A party at the Kendalls' was something to anticipate. They had a pine-paneled rumpus room, with a soft-drink bar at one end, a radio and record-player. There was always plenty of food.

Liz phoned Marcy around dinner-time to suggest that she bring along some of her newest dance records and Marcy agreed to do so. She couldn't resist the temptation to ask, "The guest of honor arrived all right this morning?"

"Yes," Liz said, "with enough luggage to last six months!"

"I take it you can talk freely?"

"Why not? She's taking a bath—using up all the hot water, too, I don't doubt. And Mom's in the kitchen."

"Is she as bad as you were afraid she'd be?"

"No," Liz said glumly, "worse. On account of the year difference in our ages, she treats me like a fugitive from a play-pen. But you'll find out soon enough for yourself. 'Bye now. . . ."

Devon Merriott proved to be one of the most strikingly beautiful girls Marcy had ever seen. Her hair was black, almost blue-black, and with a soft sheen that made her skin seem ivory pale by contrast. Her eyes were wide and dark, with long black lashes that you'd have taken for false if you'd seen them on a movie star. She had a sweet, engaging smile and perfect teeth. And her figure was of the type that Marcy had often heard Ken and his cronies refer to as "well stacked."

Devon's poise and self-assurance would have done credit to a woman of thirty. Her black linen dress with its simple off-the-shoulder neckline and wide gathered skirt made the other girls' light-colored summer dresses look childish and almost fussy. Her hair curled very short about her small, high-held head, in the newest manner. And she had a way of looking up into a boy's face, her head tilted ever so slightly to one side, that seemed to do something absolutely catastrophic to his will-power. This Marcy, as well as every other girl present, discovered before the evening was well under way.

When Devon gave Steve that look of hers, Marcy felt a heavy sense of foreboding swell within her. When she looked at Bill that way, Marcy knew Liz was experiencing the same sinking sensation. And Rosemary when Devon used it on Ken. And so on. All of the boys looked so—so fatuous somehow under Devon's practiced glance. As if they were just so many lumps of putty, waiting to be shaped however she wanted them. The thought made Marcy feel younger than she had in a long time. Younger and more helpless and—afraid.

"What you so quiet for?" Steve asked, as they were dancing.

But Marcy denied it. "I'm not. You just imagine it."

"Uh-uh," Steve argued. "And you keep looking at Liz's cousin. What you trying to do, absorb her technique?"

His tone was teasing, like it used to be before he started taking her out, when he simply used to consider her Ken's kid sister. It made Marcy mad.

She said sharply, "I should say not! I wouldn't act that way for anything in the world! As if every boy I looked at was so—so wonderful, when they're not at all, when they're just simply—boys!"

Steve gave her a little hard hug as he whirled her around to the lilting strains from the record-player. It wasn't the sort of hug you'd give anyone's kid sister. It made Marcy feel grown-up again and important and attractive. Even before Steve said, his lips almost touching her ear, so that his breath made her hair tickle a little, "At-a-girl! I don't want you looking at anyone that way but me, see?"

"Silly!" Marcy said, but her breath came faster and not simply from the exertion of the dance, either. . . .

The next day Liz called up and asked Marcy to come over. "My cousin," she said and it seemed to Marcy there was a note of concealed warning in her tone, "wants to get to know you better."

Liz and Devon were stretched out comfortably on the Kendalls' breezeway when Marcy arrived. They were drinking lemonade from a fat frosty pitcher and talking about the party. Marcy plopped down in a deck chair, took the glass Liz proffered her and felt Devon's warm glance wrap itself around her.

"So you're Marcy," she said, smiling. "I thought you were you, but I got a lot of names and faces scrambled together in my mind last night—meeting so many people all at once, you know?"

Marcy nodded. "It's kind of hard to remember a lot of new people," she agreed. But a catty little suspicion prodded her. She'd be willing to bet Devon didn't have any trouble remembering which boy was which. Marcy hoped she could also remember which was whose!

Liz said, "Devon's been telling me none of her friends in New York ever entertain at home any more. The party last night was the first one of its kind she's been to in simply ages!"

"But what do they do?" Marcy asked, interested in spite of herself.

"Oh, we go to some club or other," Devon said airily. "The Stork's my favorite. Sherman's such a darling!"

"Sherman Billingsley?" Marcy asked. "You mean you know him?"

"But, of course," Devon said. "Simply everyone knows Sherman. When our crowd goes there for a party, he's so sweet."

"Gee," Marcy said.

Liz told her, "Sometimes, just for variety, they go to

the Starlight Roof. And in the winter, there are skating parties at Rockefeller Plaza."

"Gee," Marcy said again.

The thought of anyone actually going to these glamorous places, which were just names to her, made her regard Liz's cousin with a new respect. Not envy, though. Marcy thought, as a regular thing, she would prefer skating on the lake, where you could build a big bonfire for warming up, to whipping over the perfect ice at Rockefeller Plaza, with all the big buildings shutting you in like a pocket and curious passers-by standing around to watch. And as for going to the Stork Club and actually meeting its famous proprietor—well, it would be fun for once, of course, but parties at people's houses were a lot of fun, too, and you didn't have to be so elegantly dressed and so much on your dignity. Or, at least, so it seemed to Marcy.

She sat there, talking with Devon, listening to her tell of her life in the city. Devon lived on Riverside Drive, she was familiar with buses and the subway. Broadway meant more to her than just a kaleidoscope of bright lights, that sometimes popped up as background in a movie. She often shopped at Saks Fifth Avenue, trod the maze of Grand Central Station, rode the Staten Island Ferry which passed within plain sight of the Statue of Liberty, went to Coney Island. And here she was, sitting close enough to Marcy to be touched, going out of her way, or so it seemed, to be friendly and interested.

When it was time for Marcy to go, Devon said, "You must come over again soon, mustn't she, Liz, darling?"

And Liz, who probably spent half her waking hours in Marcy's company, said drily, "As if she had to be asked!"

Marcy giggled.

"Are you two very close friends?" Devon inquired.

"Like that," Liz told her, holding up two fingers pressed tight against each other.

"But that's wonderful," Devon said. "Because I liked you the very best of all the girls who were here last night." She glanced at her cousin for corroboration. "Didn't I, Liz? Didn't I tell you so right after the party was over?"

Liz nodded morosely. "That's what you said."

"And it's true," Devon told Marcy, smiling at her sweetly, beguilingly, her head tilted just a tiny bit toward one side, her wide dark eyes shining.

Marcy didn't think she had ever met anyone quite so charming. Devon seemed much warmer and more friendly than she had last night. Evidently, Marcy told herself, she was one of those people who grew on you, whom you liked more and more as you came to know them better. If she had ever been the brat Liz described her as being, she had long since outgrown it.

"Well—well, thanks," Marcy stammered, pleased.

"I told Liz," Devon went on, "that you seemed older than the other girls someway, more sophisticated."

"Did you really?" Marcy asked, her eyes quite round.

Devon nodded. But it was Liz's voice that put in, "She liked Ken the best of all the boys who were here, too, didn't you, Devon?"

Devon gave her a cold look. "I thought he was quite attractive." She turned her attention back to Marcy with a smile. "Don't you think so?"

"Well—" Marcy's answering smile was a little doubtful, "I guess maybe he is. Only—being his sister, I just never thought of him that way."

"But Devon did," Liz reiterated.

Marcy's throat ached a little, seeing quite plainly what Liz was pointing out to her. Liz might just as well have said flatly, "Devon likes your brother so she's putting herself out to be nice to you. She wants you on her side when she goes after him."

But Liz could be mistaken, Marcy told herself. Surely Devon wouldn't be that hypocritical, pretending to like her, Marcy, just to get ahead with Ken.

Devon's smile was as warm, her eyes as shining, as they had been before. Only somehow the effect was spoiled a little by the shadow cast by Liz's doubt of her motives.

Anyway, Marcy assured herself staunchly, Ken could certainly take care of himself.

Chapter Eight

KEN MAKES A DISCOVERY

It was twelve o'clock noon on a bright July Sunday and an atmosphere of quiet peace hovered over the trim lawns and comfortable houses of Cedar Avenue in Westfield. Practically no one was about. The people who had gone to church were home looking at the Sunday papers by this time. Those who were playing golf wouldn't be back for a while yet. The lazy souls who liked to sleep late were, for the most part, just dragging themselves downstairs and trying to decide whether to bother with a regular breakfast, or wait for dinner.

George Rhodes, in a fit of rare energy, was cleaning the car. His job as sales-manager of a printing company, which had expanded to the point where it now had branches in several large cities, was mainly sedentary.

George was always complaining that he didn't get enough exercise. And cleaning the car this lovely day both kept him out in the fresh air and utilized his muscles, so George was going at it in a big way.

He had just started on the final rubbing down when Ken, who had approached silently and was standing there watching him, inquired earnestly, "Don't you need some help, Dad?"

George, exerting magnificent self-control, did not reel and clutch the car for support. He did regard his son curiously, however, as any normal father would when faced with an unprecedented development of this sort.

"Why—thanks, Ken," he remarked in as calm a voice as he could muster. "If you like. There's an extra chamois in the trunk."

Silently Ken extracted the chamois from a welter of old inner tubes and assorted tools, silently he started in polishing the hood. His father was silent, too. Patience seemed indicated. And George was practically certain that if he waited long enough, light would be vouchsafed him. Light presently was, after Ken had wielded the chamois industriously for several minutes.

"Uh—Dad, I wanted to have a little talk with you about my allowance."

Aha, George thought, but he refrained from saying it aloud. He had discovered, over a considerable period of time, that to give voice to the first word that popped into his head during a conversation with his son, was the surest way to discourage further confidences. And this he had no desire to do. In fact he had been wanting to have a serious man-to-man talk with Ken on the subject of money. It was, he felt, his duty.

"Yes," he said aloud gravely, "I think that's a good idea, son. Just how far ahead are we on it now?"

"About four weeks, I guess," Ken admitted in a slightly strangled voice. "But, golly Moses, Dad, you know I wanted to get a regular job this summer and you and Mom wouldn't let me."

"I know," his father nodded. "That's why I've been as lenient as I have in giving you some advances. But I seem to remember you saying the last time you borrowed ahead that you were going to take a cut in the amount you get each week till the extra twenty or so dollars has been made up."

"Yeah, I know," Ken said, looking stricken. "But, you see, Dad, things have come up since then—important things—stuff I didn't have any idea about when I said that."

"Such as?" George Rhodes prompted.

In the small space of time before Ken answered, his father thought: I'm not going to let him sell me a bill of goods this time. I'm going to stand firm. He gets around me too easily, yes, and his mother, too. It's not good training for him to have his finances in a perpetual state of being spread so thin he always has to borrow ahead. He's got to learn sometime to live within his income, to plan his expenditures according to his cash on hand.

"Well," Ken's uncomfortable voice broke into his father's reflections, "it's really serious this time. This is an emergency."

It was always an emergency, George reminded himself, when something Ken wanted was at stake. "Is that right?" he inquired, steeling himself against the appeal in his son's tone.

Ken nodded. "It sure is," he said hoarsely. "Y'see, Dad, it's on account of Devon that I need money. Devon Merriott—that's her whole name. She's visiting the Kendalls, she's Liz's cousin. Surely you musta seen her around."

He looked at his father hopefully for corroboration, as though, had he seen Devon with his own eyes, he would be better able to understand Ken's dilemma and more sympathetically inclined to help him with a solution.

But the older man shook his head briskly in the negative. "No, I can't say I've noticed her, son."

"Then you haven't seen her," Ken said positively. He sighed, so deeply that it seemed the sound must have come from the utmost depths of his anatomy. "Boy, is she a dish!"

His father stared at him. Always before Ken's contacts with the fair sex had been characterized by the light, not to say casual, touch. Now his blue eyes were fixed dazedly on space and a singularly inane expression had settled over all his features. He polished the same spot on the car over and over, the movement of his hand grasping the chamois purely automatic.

"I see," George said gently, but with no altering of the firmness in his tone. Love might make the world go around and Ken might be feeling its potent force for the first time, but it wasn't going to alter his father's determination to withstand any further requests for advances on Ken's allowance. He had made up his mind.

Ken said dreamily, "She's out of this world, Dad—you never saw anything like her. Black hair and sort of creamy white skin and big dark eyes that kind of—kind of—" his voice ran down.

His father nodded. "I think I know what you mean, Ken."

"And her figure's terrific," Ken went on. "And, brother, can she dance! Every guy in the crowd—or almost—is loopy about her. I've been lucky enough to get several dates with her the two weeks she's been here." His tone descended a confidential note lower. "That's why I'm so broke."

"Is she pretty expensive to take out?" his father asked.

"You said it!" Ken admitted. He added with touching

honesty, "Usually Marcy's good for a small loan when I'm in a spot. But she's broke, too—or so she says. I think maybe it's just that she doesn't like Devon very well."

"Why not?"

"Oh, you know women," Ken shrugged. "I think Marcy's got a kind of complex about her. She's convinced Devon's buttering her up on my account. But that's silly. Why should Devon be nice to my sister to get in good with me, when she can have any guy she wants?"

"I wouldn't know," George said drily. "But why do you have to spend so much money on her? She isn't what we used to call a 'gold digger' in my day, is she?"

"Oh, no," Ken denied positively. "It isn't that she expects it, or anything. But—well, the thing is, she's from New York. And she's used to going to all these swank places like the Stork Club and all. So you can't just take her to the drugstore for a soda and stuff like that, like you can the local girls. I mean, she dresses so sharp and everything, you just feel you've got to take her someplace sort of—special."

"Such as?" his father inquired.

"Well, we went out to the lake pavilion dancing a couple of times—it's nothing like she's used to, but at least there's an orchestra instead of a juke box. There haven't been any dances at the country club since Devon's been here, or we could have gone there. And a couple of times I took her over to Clay City and we saw a stage show and had dinner. Last night we just went to the movies. It was lucky I had enough cash to do that."

"I'd say so, too," George agreed. "No wonder you're broke." He made his tone very firm. "The best advice I can offer you, Ken, is to lay off asking her for any more dates till you've got your financial affairs on a sounder basis."

"But she's only going to be here till the end of the month," Ken objected. "That's just a couple of weeks."

"Even so—" his father began.

But Ken interrupted desperately, "Besides, I've already got another date with her—for Monday night. That's tomorrow," he elaborated. "And do you know what that is?"

"The tenth," his father said, after a moment's thought.

"It's Devon's birthday," Ken said portentously. "And not another fella in the crowd knows about it but me!"

His father eyed him thoughtfully for a long moment. Then he inquired, "What makes you think she hasn't announced the interesting fact to them, if she told you?"

"Aw, Dad!" Quite obviously Ken was shocked. "She's not that kind at all. Golly Moses, if you knew her you'd be ashamed you even thought things like that about her. She didn't *tell* me it was going to be her birthday."

"Then how did you find out?"

Ken proceeded to explain in detail. It seemed that the

night before, when he and Devon went to the movies, she had been wearing a locket. And, during the course of the show, the chain broke. So she gave him the locket to keep for her, since it was a trinket, she admitted, which she valued highly, it having been given to her by her parents for her birthday years and years ago.

"It wasn't till this morning," Ken admitted, "that I realized I'd forgotten to give it back to her. I still had it in my pocket. So, of course, I got to looking at it. And it was engraved inside, with her name and the date. So that's how I know tomorrow's her birthday." He hurried on optimistically, "Naturally, Dad, you can see I'd want to give her a little gift. I thought if you could just advance me my allowance that'll be due next Wednesday and maybe just a couple of dollars extra—"

"No," said George, breaking into this flow of eloquence firmly and fixing his son with a stern paternal eye.

"Aw, but, Dad," said Ken in pained surprise, "I thought you'd understand—"

"I understand, Ken," his father said. "But the answer's still 'no.' I'd like to help you, but I've gone as far as I intend to in this matter of advancing you money."

"But, Dad—"

George shook his head. "I certainly don't see there's any emergency involved here. The girl doesn't even know you know it's her birthday. So why should she expect a gift from you? No, Ken, I'm sorry, but I can't let you have a cent."

"But—"

"No," George Rhodes said again in his very most stern-father tone. And his conscience assured him he was doing nothing more than his simple duty. After all, a man has to take a stand somewhere. He had been very reasonable about Ken's earlier requests for advances. Too reasonable, maybe. That was where he'd made his mistake. But it still wasn't too late to rectify it.

"Okay, Dad," Ken sighed morosely. He hung the chamois he had been using over the car door handle and moved off toward the house. His step was heavy.

When he's older, his father thought, staring after him, he'll understand. At least, George hoped he would. He wished Ken understood right now. He wished—oh, well . . .

Ken tried Mom next. But the tenth was a bad time of the month for Mom, she always liked to get the household bills paid by then and her budget balanced. Besides, as soon as she heard Dad had turned Ken down, she felt qualms about appearing to undermine his authority. So that just left Marcy.

"No," Marcy said flatly, when Ken had stated the situation to her. "If it was Rosemary's birthday, I might help you out."

"Then you have got some money. Come on, be a good egg."

"I've got lots of things to buy with it—for me," Marcy informed him. "And I've only got a few dollars. No, I won't loan you a cent, Ken."

"Why don't you like Devon?" Ken asked. "Is it something Liz told you about her? Devon says Liz never liked her—"

"Liz would if Devon wasn't the way she is."

"What way is she?" Ken asked.

"Sly," Marcy said after a moment. "Like pretending to think I was so wonderful, till I had her over here and she was able to really get her hooks into you."

"That's bunk!" Ken said. "Why, the first time I laid eyes on her, that night at Liz's party, I thought she was the most beautiful, the most wonderful—" he broke off at Marcy's look of pitying derision. "So why would she have to work on me through you?"

"She just wasn't taking any chances," Marcy said. "Liz says that's her system. She goes after a man like a steamroller—only more subtle. Like playing up to his sister—"

"You and Liz imagine that," Ken said, slightly riled. "Devon says girls never understand her. She tries to be friends, but—"

"Friends," Marcy sniffed. "She doesn't know the meaning of friendship. You don't see her wasting any time on me now that she's got you safely in her clutches, do you? And even though she seems to like you best of all the boys, is she content merely to make Rosemary miserable? No, she's got to keep all the rest of the boys dangling, too—Bix and Don and Bill and Henry, everyone but Steve."

"At least, she didn't take him away from you," Ken said. "You ought to give her credit for that."

"Give her credit?" Marcy's eyes blazed. "Give Steve credit, you mean, for having enough sense to see through her. All she wants of any of the boys is what she can get out of them."

"Aw, you're nuts," Ken said.

"Am I? Then why do you suppose she just 'accidentally' let you find out about her birthday?"

"Well, it *was* an accident," Ken said hotly. "Or do you think she broke her locket chain on purpose?"

"I wouldn't put it past her," Marcy said, feeling a little ashamed of herself for her own suspicions. But it made her so mad, seeing Ken let Devon wind him around her little finger, while Rosemary, who was twice as sweet, really, was hopelessly crushed. Why did boys have to be so blind, so stupid? If Steve had the common sense to see through Devon's man-snatching wiles, her crafty little schemes, why couldn't Ken?

"You're loopy," Ken said. "Just plain loopy. You take Liz's word for everything and Liz and Devon never have got along."

"Well, Liz tried to be nice to her when she first came," Marcy defended her friend. "She was willing to let bygones be bygones. But Devon started right in being condescending toward her, treating her as if she were a mere child. And did she keep her hands off Bill Weaver, when she knew Liz likes him? No, Devon has to have his scalp, too. It's no wonder none of the girls like her."

"Still, Monday's her birthday," Ken said, trying to soften Marcy up. "Don't you feel even a little bit sorry for her, having a birthday when no one even knows about it, when her parents are thousands of miles away?"

"No," Marcy told him. "And do you know why? Because Devon wants it that way, she doesn't want anyone to know it's her birthday—anyone but you, I guess. Why, Mrs. Kendall knows the date Devon was born. But when she suggested that Liz invite all the girls in for a nice birthday luncheon for her, you know what Devon did? Simply turned up her nose at the whole idea, said hen parties were just too dull and birthday parties were absolutely childish. And she swore Liz and Mrs. Kendall both to secrecy about it being her birthday. So why should I feel sorry for her?"

Ken gave her a very dirty look. "Okay, Squirt, be that way if you want to. But don't go telling Liz I know it's Devon's birthday. If I am able to raise any money, I want to surprise her."

Marcy laughed airily. "Surprise her, my foot! I'll bet

she's counting on a present from you."

Ken shook his head. "And I had hopes of you developing into a human being. Remember now," he warned, "don't go hashing over my private affairs with Liz."

"What do you think I am?" Marcy inquired in an aloof tone.

She watched Ken walk away, shoulders slumped, hands thrust into pockets. A lump in her throat assumed choking proportions. But she wouldn't give in to the urge that bade her call him back and give him her few hoarded dollars. She would hold out for his own good. But it wasn't easy. . . .

Chapter Nine

KEN GETS AN IDEA

At least, Ken seemed to harbor no grudge. Only the slightest trace of patient martyrdom tinged his manner at dinner. Both his parents and Marcy studied him speculatively at one time or another during the meal to make sure. His appetite seemed in no way impaired, either, and this they took as a good sign that he wasn't brooding. All of them felt, secretly, a little guilty.

When Ken had finished the last elusive crumb of his banana-cream pie, he excused himself politely and strolled out. A few minutes later his father observed him, through the living-room window, in conference with Tom Martin, who lived next door.

"I expect," George remarked, "he's trying to line up a job. The Martins' hedge could use a little clipping."

"Tom'll probably want to do it himself, though"—Lila said. "He's getting worried about his waistline."

Her husband regarded her thoughtfully. "Did Ken touch you for a loan?"

Lila nodded. "I said 'no,' though. I backed you up."

Marcy glanced from one to the other of their slightly troubled faces. "I turned him down, too," she admitted.

"That was wise of you, dear," Mom told her. "You must realize we're only being firm with Ken for his own good."

"We don't want him to stay so irresponsible about money," Dad explained.

"I don't think he's irresponsible," Marcy said stubbornly, leaping to Ken's defense as she always felt impelled to do. "It's just that I don't like the idea of him wasting his money on that Devon. She isn't worth it."

"Why, Marcy!" Mom said in surprise. "That isn't a very nice way to talk about Liz's cousin."

"Liz can't help that," Marcy said. "We can pick our friends but our relatives get wished on us." She got up and ambled out into the hall. "I'm going up to put on my shorts. Steve and I are playing tennis later."

After a moment's thoughtful silence, George asked his wife, "Do you know this Devon, Lila?"

"Oh, yes, I've met her over at Kendalls'. She's quite beautiful, really, but just the type that makes even nice kids like Liz and Marcy arch their backs and stick out their claws a little."

"Now why would that be, I wonder?"

Lila shrugged. "There are women who affect me like that, even at my age. The sort that can't resist making a big play for any male, whether she really cares a hoot about him or not. You know what I mean?"

Her husband grinned at her. "You mean this Devon's a *femme fatale*—at seventeen?"

Lila smiled, too. "In embryo. And the fact that she's just beginning to feel her power makes her all the harder to put up with. Maybe as she grows older, she'll exercise more control. Right now she simply reaches out and grabs every boy in sight for the mere pleasure of knowing she can."

George chuckled. "No wonder all the girls are down on her."

"Poor little Rosemary's heart-broken, I guess, because it seems Devon's taken with Ken most of all. And Ken is definitely dazzled."

"Oh, all of that," George agreed. "Well, I hope he's able to earn a little money for her present. Not that I care whether she gets one or not. But the trouble is, after a certain number of accusing looks, I begin to feel like a cruel step-father."

"Me, too," Lila admitted, sighing. . . .

Playing tennis that afternoon at the park, Steve beat Marcy by a comfortable margin. Afterward they drank Cokes at the Park House and then went out and sat on the grassy bank overlooking the small lake.

"Think you'll ever amount to much as a tennis player?" Steve inquired. "You were even worse than usual this afternoon."

"You're just so good," Marcy drawled in a ludicrously saccharine manner. "What chance is there for poor little me?"

Steve mussed her hair forward over her eyes. "Can it!"

"Why?" Marcy asked, blowing her hair upward. "Devon gets away with it. What's she got that I haven't?"

Steve flopped over on his stomach and lay there, grinning up at her. "Not a thing, baby. You're quite a gal in shorts. It's a wonder I could keep my mind on the game enough to beat you, seeing all that feminine pulchritude on the other side of the net."

Marcy said, "It's my lovely golden tan. Gets 'em every time."

Steve tickled her ankle with a blade of grass. "Whatever it is, it's got me."

They lolled there, silent for a moment. But there was nothing strained or uncomfortable about their silence. Marcy had learned this spring and summer that you didn't have to chatter all the time to hold a boy's attention and interest. Steve liked her to be herself, to talk or be quiet according to her mood, to say what she thought, not what she thought he wanted her to say. He liked her as a person, an individual, just as she liked him. There was a friendship and understanding between them and just a little more, an added something that made her heart bump when he held her hand, or sometimes when his breath tickled her ear as they were dancing. A spark, a warmth, that might or might not develop into something stronger and more lasting. But it gave a lift to their relationship which was missing when she dated other boys, no matter how fine a time they showed her. And there was no need to give a name to it, no need at all.

From herself and Steve, Marcy's thoughts went on to Ken and Rosemary—and Devon. Rosemary was putting the best face possible on the situation, pretending she didn't care and not fooling anyone. Even though Ken had played the field, Rosemary was the girl he dated most often, the one he kept coming back to. And now —it must be dreadfully hard for her, Marcy thought, to see Ken so completely under Devon's spell. If it were Steve, she knew how she'd feel. She felt bad enough, goodness knows, seeing Ken act so silly—

"What you thinking about?" Steve asked.

"Oh—mostly Ken and Devon."

"Boy, that's a Thing, isn't it?" Steve wagged his head.

"Old Ken sure swallowed hook, line and sinker."

"If he tries to borrow any money from you—" Marcy began

But Steve interrupted. "If? He already has."

"Today you mean?" Marcy asked. And then, at Steve's nod, "Did you loan him any?"

Steve shook his head sadly. "I got barely enough to see me through. Money sure goes fast these days. What's Ken need it for, another date with glamor-puss?"

"Something like that," Marcy said, remembering Ken's admonition to keep mum on his private affairs. "But none of us at home would help him out, either. Now he's out trying to line up some lawns to mow or something."

Steve said, "I hope he has better luck than I did. Seems as if everybody's doing their own yard work these days."

"Poor Ken," Marcy said pityingly. . . .

At breakfast the next morning, Ken asked, "Mind if I ride uptown with you, Dad? Thought I'd see if the Market could use me today."

"Why, of course, son," his father said. "You didn't get anything lined up yesterday, I take it?"

Ken shook his head. "That's always the way. When you feel like taking it easy, everybody wants his lawn rolled or his hedge barbered. But when you need a job—" he left it at that and went mournfully back to his oatmeal.

Marcy, spreading her buttered toast liberally with

strawberry jam, felt at the same time relieved and regretful. Sorry for Ken, but glad she had had the foresight last night, when she was in the drugstore with Liz, to spend practically her last cent on a king-sized bottle of perfume with an unpronounceable French name and a most alluring fragrance. Now if Ken tried to wheedle some money from her, she could say truthfully she didn't have any.

Mom came in from the kitchen with the percolator in her hand, just in time to hear Ken's last words. She suggested, "You might try Uncle Matt, Ken. Sometimes he can use some temporary help around the greenhouse."

"Yeah," Ken said, "I thought of him."

As a matter of fact, Uncle Matt was his ace in the hole, his last resort. Ken had had him in mind long before Mom mentioned him. But first, after saying goodbye to his father at the corner of Second and Main Streets, he tried the Market. Mr. Storm, the manager, couldn't use any extra help on Monday, though. He told Ken so, regretfully. In rapid succession then and with uniformly unsuccessful results, Ken tried the drugstore and radio shop. Sometimes one of these business enterprises needed an extra delivery boy. But not today.

Mid-morning found him beginning to get both footsore and hungry, as he made his way into Cameron Flower Shop. The moist fragrant coolness was a relief after the heat of the street outside. Matt Cameron was arranging roses in a tall vase at the counter.

"Well, hello, Ken," his uncle, a genial rosy-cheeked little man like a younger beardless Santa Claus, welcomed him. "Want to buy another orchid for a fair lady?"

Ken's grin was feeble. "In my present financial state, I couldn't buy a daisy."

Uncle Matt shook his head. "Too bad. This is a slow season for the florist business. Everybody's got too many flowers growing in their back yards, I guess." He gestured toward a sign in the window, SPECIAL SALE ON ROSES. "Even that doesn't move 'em."

Ken's heart hit his heels with a dull thud. "I stopped by to see if you could use any extra help for a day or so. I sure need a job bad."

He had to ask, hopeless as it seemed. Maybe Uncle Matt would take pity on him. Blood was supposed to be thicker than water—but after the way his own family had let him down, Ken doubted it.

Sure enough, Uncle Matt shook his head sadly from side to side. "That's too bad, Ken. I wouldn't have a thing for you. Willie and I are twiddling our thumbs around here as it is."

Ken sighed. There went his last hope.

"I'm sorry," Uncle Matt said.

"It's okay," Ken told him. "If you could, you would." He stood around for a few minutes more, talking, then said good-bye.

A feeling of futility and hopelessness settled over him as he closed the door. Despite the bright sunshine, the day seemed grim and gray. Ken noticed Bix Meyers' butter-yellow convertible parked down the block. Morosely he moved toward it, climbed in and slumped down till his knees bumped the dashboard.

Ken sat for quite a while, thinking. When in the throes of serious thought, he always squinted his eyes, screwed up his forehead and set his jaw pugnaciously. Life, it seemed to him at the moment, was scarcely what you could call worth while. Where was the general appreciation of industry and ambition he had always been led to suppose existed? Yeah, where?

Money, Ken thought—who was it said it wasn't the most important thing in the world? Of course, maybe it was only important when you didn't have it. And at that, maybe love was more important. Only somehow love and money seemed to sort of hinge on each other.

Ken sighed again. He had to get some money. No money, no birthday present for Devon. His thoughts ran in a futile circle. Still—as this angle occurred to him, he brightened a bit—although he might not be able to give her anything, at least he had the satisfaction of knowing that none of the other guys in the crowd could surprise her, either. None of them knew anything about the portentous date. That was something—or was it? Maybe he was looking at the matter in the wrong way. Morosely

Ken pondered some more.

Presently Bix Meyers ambled into his line of vision. Bix's brass-colored hair glowed in the sun, his violently printed sport shirt would have been right at home in California. He was whistling as if he didn't have a care in the world. Maybe he hadn't, Ken mused. Some guys had all the luck.

"Hi!" Bix broke off his tune to hail Ken cheerfully.

"Hi," answered Ken. There was a look of speculation in his eye. He moved over to give Bix room to slide in under the wheel.

"Want to go someplace special?" Bix asked. "Or just home?"

Ken merely raised his brows and continued to regard his friend in a thoughtfully appraising manner.

"What's eating you?" asked Bix, who was a forthright soul. "You mad 'cause I got a date with Devon tomorrow night?"

Ken shook his head. "I got a date with her tonight," he informed Bix. "And that brings up a very interesting subject." He leaned confidentially closer. "You got any money?"

"Me?" inquired Bix, his manner cooling perceptibly. "Why?"

"I'd like to—uh—borrow some."

"That's a good one," said Bix with a decidedly nasty laugh. "I should loan you money to make a big impression on the girl I'm going to take out tomorrow night. I should be an anti-climax in her life. You think I got a hole in my head?"

"It would be a noble gesture."

"Maybe," Bix said, "but I'm a stinker. Besides, fella, I haven't got any more cash than it'll take for my date with her."

Ken sighed. "Somehow I felt you'd say that." He relapsed into brooding silence. A moment later, however, when he brought his gaze to rest on Bix again, there was a friendly tolerance in his eye. "It's okay," he said in a mildly plaintive tone. "I can't really say I blame you. Money's hard to come by. I know!"

"Attaboy," exclaimed Bix relievedly. "No hard feelings?"

Ken shook his head. "We're pals, Bix," he said solemnly, "and the way I look at it, what are pals for if not to help each other out? Right?"

"Yeah, but—" began Bix a shade uncertainly.

"Wait," Ken said, and he lowered his tone to a very confidential pitch indeed. "It just so happens I know something you'd be interested in, Bix. A lotta guys would, but, after all, we're friends, so—" he put his lips even closer to Bix's ear, "do you know when Devon's birthday is?"

"No." Bix swiveled around to stare at him. "Do you?"

"Today," breathed Ken in a voice fraught with importance. "And I'll tell you something else. It so happens I know exactly what she wants, too. So naturally that was what I was going to buy for her, but—I'm flat. I've tried to get a job and I've tried to borrow money. No soap. So I figure, if I can't take advantage of what I know, you might as well. Now I'll tell you, Bix, it's like this . . ."

Chapter Ten

DEVON CELEBRATES HER BIRTHDAY

At two o'clock that afternoon, sunlight streamed through the broad west window of the Kendalls' living-room. Devon Merriott, her lovely dark head bent over the delicate task of manicuring her fingernails, made an entrancing picture, curled up bonelessly in a deep green chair. A few feet away Liz and Marcy sat sprawled on the couch, looking anything but entranced. Liz wore faded blue pedal-pushers and a plaid gingham shirt, Marcy a sun-dress of rather limp seersucker. But Devon, even on a Monday afternoon with no other guests expected, was garbed in a crisp yellow piqué skirt and white peasant blouse, with matching yellow sandals on her slim feet.

"You know," said Devon, "I've just been thinking.

Now that I'm seventeen, I really ought to take a more—well, a deeper sort of attitude toward living. After all, I'm not a child any more."

"Who's a child?" Liz inquired a shade belligerently. "I'll be seventeen myself in eight months."

"I'll be in eleven," Marcy added, but somehow it didn't sound very impressive.

"I didn't mean you, darlings," Devon said soothingly. "But—I don't know—somehow seventeen seems so—so much more mature than sixteen, don't you think?"

"No," said Liz candidly.

And Marcy put in, "I don't see why a year one way or the other should make so much difference."

"You look—and act," Liz informed her cousin, "just the same as you did yesterday. Being seventeen doesn't show a bit."

Devon sighed. "You just don't understand—" she began.

The door-bell chimed suddenly and Devon broke off. Her glance met her cousin's inquiringly.

Liz asked, "You expecting anyone?"

Devon shook her head. "Not till tonight. I've got a date with Ken at eight."

Marcy knew about that. But even Ken, loopy as he was over Devon, wouldn't arrive this early. Not six hours!

The girls sat listening as Mrs. Kendall went from the kitchen to answer the door-bell's repeated summons.

"I wonder—" began Devon, running smoothing fingers over her soft hair in a movement purely automatic and as old as time. Voices came from the hall—Mrs. Kendall's and—a man's! Devon stuffed her nail file and bottle of polish down behind the chair cushion and leaped for the nearest mirror.

"It's probably somebody selling something," Liz said, but she sounded a little uneasy. She tucked the tail of her plaid shirt into her pedal-pushers just in case. And Marcy smoothed down her crumpled frock and sat up a little straighter.

When Bix Meyers came into the room a moment later, Devon was seated langorously on the green chair, a magazine open across her knees. And the glance she turned in his direction was prettily compounded of surprise and pleasure. Liz and Marcy looked just a little stunned. But Bix didn't appear to notice them.

"Why—Bix!" Devon drawled throatily. "How sweet of you to drop in like this."

None of the girls could miss the large green package Bix bore so carefully. Liz's glance met Marcy's meaningfully. Liz's look said "I told you so" as plainly as her lips could have spoken it.

"Well—" Bix's customary glib wit seemed to desert him entirely in Devon's heady presence. His eyes glazed in sudden, almost paralyzing embarrassment as he managed to hand Devon the package. Finally, blushing, he achieved, "Just a little—uh—remembrance—uh—happy birthday, Devon."

"Why, Bix, how perfectly sweet of you!" exclaimed Devon in a tone of thrilled mystification. With eager fingers she loosened the strings that tied the long box, opened the lid, folded back the layers of waxed paper that shrouded Bix's offering. "O-o-oh, roses! Why, I simply adore roses, Bix. This is too perfectly wonderful of you, really, but—how did you know it's my birthday?"

"I don't suppose you told him?" said Liz, her claws showing a little.

"Why, Liz!" exclaimed Devon, turning hurt dark eyes in her cousin's direction. "I certainly didn't! Did I, Bix? You tell her."

Bix wagged his head in the negative. "It was intuition on my part," he said expansively, beginning to sound more like himself. "Maybe I'm psychic."

"Well, I think it's just wonderful," Devon informed him solemnly. "Smell them, Marcy, Liz—aren't they gorgeous?"

Marcy and Liz, after deeply appreciative sniffs, had to admit that this was so.

"It's so original of you, too, Bix," Devon went on, cradling the roses in her arms. "I mean I think it's very sophisticated, sending a girl flowers. It's the sort of thing an older man would think of doing. I'll just ask my aunt to find a vase for these—" she got gracefully to her feet—"and be right back. Do sit down, Bix, and let Liz and Marcy entertain you."

Just as Bix sat, beaming fatuously from all this flattery, the door-bell chimed again. . . .

At five o'clock when Devon's Uncle Jim arrived home, his wife waylaid him in the hallway, her face flushed and a light of near-distraction in her usually serene gaze.

"Jim," she whispered urgently, grasping him firmly by the arm and leading him toward the back of the house, "I have to talk to you. I'm nearly crazy."

"What on earth—" began Jim Kendall, but his wife shook her head and propelled him inexorably kitchenwards. As they passed the living-room door, loud, cheerful voices and hearty young laughter drifted out and engulfed them. Once in the kitchen, Helen Kendall released her hold and her husband stared at her inquiringly.

"Sounds like a party going on in there."

His wife pressed her fingers hard against her temples. "I don't know," she said. "I really don't know just what is going on. If they'd all arrived together—or if we'd invited them—then I'd have known it was going to be a mob scene and I'd have shooed them all down to the rumpus room. But it was insidious—"

"What," her husband demanded, "are you talking about?"

"Jim—" his wife clutched his arm once more, "it's Devon. Or maybe I'm doing her an injustice. Maybe it isn't her fault. Maybe it's just a wave of insanity that's affecting every boy in Liz's crowd. Because, surely, Jim, even Devon wouldn't hint seven boys into bringing her flowers—"

Jim Kendall's brow knit and his mouth dropped open a little in amazement.

"Roses," his wife went on succinctly. "Seven boys have arrived at this house since two o'clock with bright shining faces and roses—for Devon. I know it's her birthday, but, Jim, why would they all bring roses? Does it make sense to you?"

Jim shook his head, mystified.

"I'm about frantic," Helen Kendall admitted. "I've used all my vases and I sent Marcy over to borrow some from her mother and now they're all filled. I've even got roses in the cookie jar. It's like a nightmare. And now it's dinner-time and all those boys are still here and they're too old to tell to go home—although how I'd love doing it!"

"Don't you worry," Jim patted her shoulder soothingly. "Leave it to me. I'll just go in the living-room and kind of make my presence felt and pretty soon those overgrown kids'll realize their fathers must be getting home now, too." He shook his head wonderingly, an amused gleam brightening his eye. "I guess we just don't appreciate what potent stuff Devon is, Helen. Seven bouquets of roses in one afternoon—great Scott!"

It was past five-thirty when Marcy got home.

Her mother's voice reached her as soon as the screen-door slammed. "Marcy, is that you?"

"Uh-huh," Marcy said. She went out to the kitchen and hovered in the doorway.

Her mother's glance met hers curiously. "Did any more boys bring flowers since you came over for the vases?"

"Only one," Marcy said, "Don Hayworth. Mrs. Kendall put his roses in the cookie jar."

"How many was that all together?"

Marcy told her.

Lila shook her head. "It's the queerest thing I ever heard of. It couldn't have been mere coincidence."

"It wasn't," Marcy said. "Naturally the boys got to comparing notes before the afternoon was over. And you know what? It turned out Ken told them all that today was Devon's birthday and that she was simply crazy about roses."

"Ken did?" Lila repeated, frowning. "But I don't understand—"

"Neither do I," Marcy said, "but I mean to find out. Where is he?"

"Upstairs taking a bath," Mom admitted. "He wasn't even over there, though, this afternoon, was he?"

Marcy shook her head. "He was conspicuous by his absence. I've got some questions to ask him." She turned and made her way determinedly toward the stairs.

The sound of splashing water and Ken's voice lifted in slightly off-key song smote her ears as she reached the upper hall. Marcy banged on the bath-room door and the singing ceased.

"Go 'way," Ken said. "Use the powder-room."

"I want to talk to you."

"Why?" Ken asked.

"I want to find out why you told every fella in the crowd that today was Devon's birthday and that she simply loved roses."

"Most girls do," Ken said mildly. "Don't tell me Devon's an exception."

"Ken," Marcy warned, "I'm going to pop with curiosity. Why did you do it?"

"How many roses did she get?" inquired Ken maddeningly.

"Seven bunches," Marcy said. "Some big, some little."

"Zowie!" Ken exclaimed. "I didn't draw a single blank. Every guy I told swallowed the bait."

"But why?"

Ken said, in his best Sherlock Holmes voice, "It should be elemental, even to one of your limited intelligence and deductive powers, my dear Watson. To put it simply, I was talking with our mutual friend Bix Meyers this morning when suddenly I had a brain-storm. I was broke, as you no doubt remember, but I was also the only guy around who knew today was Devon's birthday. And furthermore, I have an uncle in the flower business. You begin to see light?"

"Well—sort of—" Marcy groped, "but—"

"Tsk, tsk," came from beyond the closed door. "I'm surprised at your stupidity. It was simply a matter of putting a bug in Bix's ear and then, while he was on his way to the flower shop, hot-footing it into the drug-store and calling up Uncle Matt. He was the soul of co-operation, said he'd be glad to pay me a commission on any customers I sent in. Naturally I asked him to keep our little arrangement under his hat. And he had no idea all the roses were being bought for the same girl."

"Ken, you didn't!" Marcy dissolved into laughter.

An answering chuckle reached her ears. "I was kind of busy this morning, looking up all the guys who've got a crush on Devon and telling them my little secret."

"But didn't they suspect?"

"Nah," Ken said. "First I touched 'em for a loan and after they'd turned me down, it seemed plausible enough for me to tell 'em what I knew, since I didn't have the dough to take advantage of it myself. Besides, I'm a good actor, convincing and all that."

"You're a stinker," Marcy said, but there was grudging admiration in her tone. "You collect your commission yet?"

"A little better than three bucks," Ken admitted. "Easiest cash I ever earned."

"Yeah, but all the fellas are sore at you."

"Very sore?" Ken asked.

"Well—at first they were. You should have seen each one of their faces when he first turned up, all weighed down with roses, and thinking he was putting over something very smart. And then when he saw the other boys there—and all the roses accumulating—" Marcy giggled —"it was really a scream, Ken. And then it turned into a sort of party, really, and everyone had so much fun—"

"Enough to make 'em put away the axes they'd been sharpening up for me?"

"Well, not entirely," Marcy said. "But I don't think they'll hold a permanent grudge."

"Okay," Ken said, "that's all I want to know. Go 'way now and quit disturbing me. My water's getting cold."

But Marcy had no intention of going away yet. "Ken?"

"Now what?" he yelled above his splashing.

"What are *you* going to give Devon for her birthday?"

"That's a moot question," Ken admitted. "Very moot. You see, if I spend the three bucks for a present, then I won't have any dough to take her to a show or anything. And if I spend the three bucks on entertaining her —no present. It's a vicious circle any way you look at it."

Marcy could see that it was. She stood silent in the hallway, scuffing one moccasin back and forth across the carpet, thinking. She felt just the teeniest bit guilty about Devon. It hadn't been quite fair, the way she and Liz had suspected Devon of telling all the boys the date of her birthday. Devon hadn't done that, at all. Maybe, Marcy thought, she and Liz had been just a little hard on Devon, at least in their private opinions. Maybe she'd been a little hard on Ken, too, Marcy reflected, refusing to loan him a few miserable dollars when he asked her to, spending it all on a bottle of perfume instead. Look at the times he'd helped her out when she was in a jam, the way he'd always stood by her. Why, she might never have got to know Steve, really know him, that is, if he and Ken hadn't been such good friends. A sense of desolation sent a shiver along Marcy's spine at the thought. Suddenly she made up her mind.

"Ken?" she said again.

The splashings beyond the door ceased once more. "Are you still out there, for Pete's sake?"

"I was just thinking," Marcy said. "I've got a brand-new bottle of perfume I just bought last night. I haven't even opened it. Do you—s'pose Devon might like that for her birthday?"

There was a sound of Ken's heels thudding on the bath mat and a moment later he came out, wrapped in his terry-cloth robe and with his hair sticking up in wet points all over his head. His face had an eager, hopeful sort of look. But he asked doubtfully, "Perfume? Isn't that a good deal like—roses?"

"Well, they both smell," Marcy admitted, giggling. But almost at once she sobered. She said, "You could take it back to Mr. Simms at the drugstore. I'm sure he'd exchange it for something else. A—a compact, maybe? She might like that."

Ken said, his voice just a little gruff, "Gee, Marce, you mean it? You wouldn't mind?"

Marcy said sharply, "I'm still not sure she's worth it. You're the one I'm doing it for. I can't stand seeing you going around with your chin dragging on the floor any longer."

"What a woman!" Ken said, giving her a bear hug. "What a sister!"

"Ken, let me go!" Marcy squealed. "I'll change my mind if you don't."

The front door opened and their father came in, just in time to hear the sound of their scuffling. "Are you two fighting again?" he called. "If so, stop it."

"Fighting?" Ken said. "Nothing of the sort. We just signed a truce for all time. Say, Dad," he asked then, "can I use the car tonight?"

"Why, I guess so," his father said. "Unless your mother wants to go somewhere."

"Not I," Ken heard his mother call from the kitchen.

"Boy, oh, boy," he said. "This must be my day!"

Devon was actually ready when Ken reached the Kendalls' that night. She let him in herself, giving him a slim white hand for a moment's soul-stirring pressure. "Hello, Ken."

"Gee, Devon," Ken's admiring glance took in her pale green dress, "you look sharp."

"Do I really, Ken?"

"Uh-huh!" Ken said emphatically. He asked then, "Have you been having a nice birthday?"

"How," Devon demanded, "did you know about it? And another thing I want to find out—"

"Take it easy," Ken said. "Maybe I'll explain later. But right now I've got something for you." Reaching into the pocket of his sport jacket, he extracted a small flat box.

Devon said relievedly, "At least, it's not roses." She proceeded to open the little box and her eyes widened. "O-o-oh, a compact!" she exclaimed delightedly. "How perfectly darling, Ken. And how sweet of you to think of bringing it—for me. It's so—original, too. I mean, it's just the sort of gift an older man would think of giving. I like flowers well enough, but—" her dark glance met Ken's and they both started to laugh.

"I know just what you mean," Ken said. He felt wonderful. With the car parked out in front and enough money in his pocket to take Devon to the best stage show in Clay City—well, what more could you ask? Aloud he said, "Let's get going. I don't like to slam your birthday presents or anything, but honestly, it smells like a funeral around here."

Chapter Eleven

KEN GETS SINGED

The closer loomed Devon's departure for home, the lower Ken's spirits sagged. Although her attitude toward him remained unchanged, the black shadow of their imminent separation blotted out his pleasure in their friendship. Misery dogged him. He couldn't enjoy their association for brooding over how soon it must end. Not that this seemed to bother Devon much. She was full of happy plans for the future, for the resuming of her life in New York, her return to gay familiar haunts.

"Aren't you going to miss Westfield at all?" Ken demanded one night as they were walking home from the movies.

"This funny little town?" Devon said airily. "I couldn't bear to really live here. Of course, it's all right for a visit."

"Lots of people feel that way about New York," Ken told her. "Dad always says that when he gets back from business trips."

Devon shrugged. "It gets in your blood, though—all the movement and color and excitement. I love it."

Ken caught her fingers as they walked along, held them curled close in his. "Aren't you going to miss me just a little?"

"Of course, Ken," Devon's tone was warm. "I'm going to miss you a lot. We've had fun, even though there isn't much of anything to do here."

They had danced at the lake pavilion. They had gone to stage shows in Clay City. They had seen movies in Westfield. And even though Devon could dismiss all these amusements so lightly, they had cost Ken money. His finances had taken an awful walloping this past month. But Devon was worth it. Well worth it. The thought of the rest of the summer stretching ahead bleakly without her—Ken held her hand tighter.

He said, "I wish you were staying longer. There'll be the fall dance at the country club later on."

Devon sniffed. "I never heard of a club that has so few dances. I mean what good's a club if they don't have a lot of dances?"

"You can play golf there," Ken defended. "And tennis, and there's the pool."

Devon sighed. "I'd rather dance."

After a moment Ken said, his voice a little hurt, "I'm sorry you've been so bored."

"Oh, but, Ken," Devon said, pressing her head momentarily against his shoulder, "you haven't bored me. Not for a minute. It's just the town. And Liz and some of her friends seem so immature."

"Oh, well," Ken said, mollified and also a little dizzy from the fragrant softness of her hair against his cheek, "so long as it isn't me."

They strolled on through the moon-dappled shadows of the trees, hand in hand, quiet. Ken's thoughts spun off into a long enticing day-dream. Maybe when he was through school and college, he would go east to work. Maybe he could get a terrific job of some sort in New York. Maybe he'd have a convertible and plenty of money to take Devon all the glamorous places she was accustomed to. He could see them now, dancing to the rhythm of a big-name band, strolling up Fifth Avenue, stopping to admire the fountain in the Rockefeller Plaza. All the New York landmarks he'd seen in news-reels merged in his mind into a picturesque montage, with Devon and himself moving through them. A little older, but not too much. Not enough to really change them. Maybe he wouldn't go to college, maybe he'd discover that he had some sort of unusual talent that would earn a fortune in a few months, a year at most. Maybe—

"We're here," Devon was saying, "we're home, Ken.

You're walking right past the house."

"Oh," Ken made the return trip to Westfield so fast he felt confused for a moment, unable to get his bearings. "Oh, so we are. I was just kind of—thinking."

"What about?" Devon asked softly, pausing in the deeper shadow cast by the maples near the hedge. "About —us, Ken?"

"Well, yeah," Ken said. "And about the future."

"I'd rather concentrate on right now," Devon told him. She moved a little closer and Ken took her a trifle awkwardly into his arms. She lifted her face in the shadowy darkness and their lips met and clung for a moment.

"You're sweet," Devon said then, reaching up to pat his cheek. "Very sweet. How am I going to manage to forget you?"

"Don't talk like that," Ken said in a strangled voice. "Gee, Devon, can't you persuade your folks to let you stay longer?"

Devon was shaking her head. "Oh, I wouldn't want to do that. I'm looking forward to going home, really."

"But we won't be seeing each other," Ken said miserably. "Not for a long while."

"Maybe never," Devon said. "How do we know our paths will cross again?"

"They will," Ken said positively. "They've got to! As soon as I get through school—"

"It sounds such a long time," Devon murmured, lifting her face again.

Her lips were firm and sweet under his. Ken could feel his heart hammering. Could Devon feel it, too?

"Ummmm," Devon said dreamily.

Ken held her close, his cheek against her hair. "Devon—"

"Yes?"

"Will you write to me as soon as you get home?"

After a moment, Devon said, "I don't see much point in that."

"But—" Ken's tone was pleading, "I figured we'd write each other often, every day or so."

"Oh, no," Devon said firmly, "I couldn't do that. Besides, trying to drag things out would only spoil it all."

"Spoil it?"

"Letters—" Devon shrugged. "They're so unsatisfactory. You can't hold hands with a letter, or kiss it. And usually they're quite dull."

"Well, thanks," Ken said drily.

"I don't just mean your letters," Devon told him. "I mean in general. After we'd been apart a little while, what would we have to write about?"

"I'd have lots of things—" Ken began.

But Devon interrupted airily, "I'd keep putting off answering. And that would make you mad."

"But—" Ken groped unhappily, "do you mean that when you leave day after tomorrow, that'll just be the end?"

Devon nodded. "It's the best way."

"But I've got to see you again. If I come to New York—"

Devon stood a little apart from him then. "Don't, Ken." Her voice was gentle, but with a note of finality in it.

"Don't what?"

"Fool yourself," Devon said. "You won't come to New York. I'm enough of a realist to admit I wouldn't want you to."

Ken was quiet for a moment. He could see Devon's eyes glitter in the moonlight. A cold glitter, ice-hard. Or did he imagine that? He asked, "You mean—I wouldn't fit in with your friends there?"

Devon said, "To be perfectly frank, no. They're—older, smoother, they know their way around. You're fine in Westfield, but—"

"Gee, thanks," Ken said bitterly. His voice rasped a little, "Don't lose any sleep worrying for fear I might turn up sometime and embarrass you."

"Don't be like that," Devon coaxed. "Can't we just be a nice memory for each other?" She made a little movement toward him, but Ken backed away.

Having taken the first few steps, the next ones came easier. . . .

After Devon had gone back to New York, Marcy felt an ineffable relief. It wasn't so much that she disliked Devon as that she had never quite trusted her. And she had sensed in her a power to hurt Ken, really hurt him in some deep lasting way that he might never get over. Only having known her a month, his feelings couldn't be too deeply involved, Marcy kept reassuring herself.

When her mother asked, "Have you noticed the way Ken's moping around, Marcy?" She had to admit that she had.

"It's that Devon," she said. "They were really quite a case."

"But shouldn't he be getting over her?" Mom asked, her frown troubled. "He hasn't dated Rosemary or any other girl since Devon left."

"Give him time," Marcy said, with more confidence than she felt. "He'll forget her."

Only a few days later Rosemary was the one Marcy was consoling. Rosemary's blue eyes were desolate beneath her curly red-gold bang, her mouth drooped despondently. "Honestly, Marce, I could just die!" Rosemary wailed. "Ken doesn't even know I'm alive any more —or else he doesn't care."

"Sure he does," Marcy tried to reassure her, "or he will when he's himself again."

"When'll that be?" Rosemary asked. "I've got a perfectly good shoulder for him to weep on. I'm the sympathetic type, and how I'd love to help him forget her if he'd give me a chance."

"Maybe you're too willing," Marcy said thoughtfully.

"You mean I should play hard to get—with Ken?" Rosemary's laugh was hollow. "If he even noticed, he'd know darned well I was fooling. No, I'd better just be myself and hope for the best."

"Yes," Marcy agreed, "I guess you're right. . . ."

Ken and his depressed frame of mind were the subject of still another conversation, one which took place between his parents one night in the privacy of their bedroom. Lila was brushing her hair and George, who was already in bed, lay regarding her thoughtfully for a while before bringing up the question which had been troubling him.

"Lila," he said, "what do you think we can do to get Ken out of his doldrums? It's been two weeks since that girl left and he hasn't snapped out of it yet. It's not like him to take any female that seriously."

"Devon," Lila admitted, "is apparently no ordinary female. But I think Ken will be all right. From different things he and Marcy have said, I've got the impression that he isn't only trying to throw off the effects of first love, but that he's been hurt and disillusioned a bit, too."

Her husband nodded. "It's got to happen to every kid sometime, I suppose. But I wish there was something we could do, some way—" his voice trailed off.

"I was thinking," Lila said, "about that long bike trip he and Steve Judson were talking about last winter. If he got away for a while maybe it would do him good."

"It might at that," George agreed. "Where were they thinking of going, do you remember?"

"Oh, north," Lila said, "up through Wisconsin, maybe even across the Canadian border. They figured on taking three or four weeks, stopping at hostels on the way."

George nodded thoughtfully. "Sounds like a good idea. I'd be willing to finance a trip like that for Ken, if he still wants to take it."

"Oh, I think he does," Lila said. "He and Steve were both awfully keen on it last winter. I'll feel Ken out. . . ."

Ken, it seemed, was definitely still interested in taking a bike trip through the north woods. When he heard that his father was willing to finance the project, his eagerness mounted still higher. Armed with the maps on which he and Steve had plotted their possible course during the long winter evenings when the idea had first occurred to them, he sought his friend out. But Steve, to Ken's stunned astonishment, seemed to have lost his first fine enthusiasm for the excursion.

"How come?" Ken demanded. "What gives with you? I thought you were all for it."

"Well, yeah," Steve admitted, "I was—last winter. But when school was out and we didn't talk any more about it—well, I figured it was all off."

"Now why would you figure that way?" Ken asked. "We've been pretty busy since school was out. This is the first chance we've had to get around to the trip."

Both of them knew Ken had been busy with Devon Merriott. But Steve had no desire to make Ken unhappy by dragging her into the conversation. He said, "Yeah, but, gee, Ken, the summer's half gone. School will be starting again in five weeks."

"That's okay," Ken argued. "Let's finish vacation off in a blaze of glory. I can just smell those pine trees, see the sparkling turquoise water of all those lakes—"

"Feel the Charley horse we'll get from all that bike pedaling?" Steve asked drily. "Or don't they mention such things in the travel folders?"

"Your outlook's warped," Ken told him. "A shame, too, in one so young. What's happened to all your youthful enthusiasm? Why, you were as keen as I was when we first got the idea—" he broke off to eye Steve questioningly. "Is it money? Don't you think your father'd come through?"

Steve considered this. "Yeah," he had to admit, "I kinda think he would. All that outdoor life would strike him as a good healthy thing for me."

"Well, then, why are you hanging back? We could have a heck of a swell time, Steve. And honestly, I'm kind of sick of things around here. A change would do me good."

"You maybe, but what about me?" Steve asked. "I'm not sick of anything. I haven't had any girl trouble. In fact, this has been just about the best summer I can remember."

Ken stared at him blankly. Then the dawn of unwilling comprehension burst upon him. "You don't mean—because of my sister? You haven't soured on our trip because of Marcy?"

"Well, why not? She's quite a girl, Ken. Don't sell her short just because you're related. Lots of guys I know would give their eye-teeth to stand where I do with her."

Ken held his head in both hands. "Not Marcy! Not my little kid sister that you've known ever since she wore—well, anyway you've known her too long to go that loopy over her!"

"Look who's talking about guys going loopy," Steve said. "If I ever saw anybody fall so hard he bounced—"

"Okay," Ken said hastily, "let's skip the comparisons. But what I'm getting at is this, just what do you think will happen with Marcy if you're gone a few weeks?"

"It'd be murder," Steve said simply. "Some wolf'd grab her for sure. A man's got to stick around to keep his claim staked out. No, the trip's off so far as I'm concerned." He added then, in what Ken supposed he intended for a consoling tone, "But after all, you can get any number of guys who'd get a kick out of going with you—unattached guys, that is. Don't look like I've scuttled the whole deal."

Shades of Romeo and Juliet, Ken thought a trifle wildly. When he had held the match that lit the flame in Steve's and Marcy's respective hearts, he'd certainly had no idea of starting a forest fire like this!

Chapter Twelve

THE BIKE TRIP

Lila Rhodes was engaged in the delicate operation of browning the meringue on a lemon cream pie, when she heard the front door slam and Ken's voice announcing, "Hi, Mom. It's me." So intent was she on her task that it wasn't until she had taken the pie from the oven and set it, with justifiable pride, aside to cool, that the realization struck her that something must be wrong. With Ken, not the pie.

Usually his arrivals home were attended with sound and upheaval. He dropped whatever he happened to be carrying, such as tennis racquet or ping-pong paddle, tripped over the coffee table or bumped resoundingly into a chair as he made his way straight to the kitchen, sniffing like a setter pup and demanding, "What's cookin'?"

But this afternoon all was silence. After that initial door slam, that greeting which, Lila realized belatedly, had certainly lacked Ken's usual verve, no sound had crashed or clattered or resounded through the house. And Ken hadn't come out to the kitchen, despite the enticing aroma of lemon cream pie.

Unquestionably something was wrong. Lila hurried into the living-room, her nose smudged with flour and a troubled frown above her blue eyes. Ken sat slumped on the couch, his long legs in the inevitable blue jeans thrust out before him. He had spilled something that looked like chocolate soda down the front of his white tee-shirt. This combined with the shock of hair bristling over his forehead and his despondent expression gave him a little-boy look that his mother found curiously touching.

"Ken, what's the matter?" Lila asked.

Ken managed to struggle up from the depths of his morose absorption sufficiently to answer. "Everything's the matter, that's what! That Steve! What a double crosser!"

"Steve?" Lila repeated incredulously. "What's he done?"

"Our bike trip's all off," Ken said broodingly. "Steve let me down without batting an eyelash."

His mother stared at him, frowning. How could that be, she wondered? For weeks last winter Ken and Steve had sprawled on their stomachs in this very room, surrounded by a litter of road maps, travel folders, lists of equipment and such. Lila had stumbled over their legs and picked up after them and lent a sympathetic ear to their endless discussion of itinerary and cost, of the hostels at which they would stay and the terrific time they would have. And now— She asked, baffled, "But why, Ken? I thought he was just as keen on the idea as you."

"Not any more, he isn't." Ken's chest, under the chocolate-stained tee-shirt, heaved with his sigh. "And do you know why he's soured on the trip?" At his mother's gesture of denial, he went on, "Because of none other but my esteemed sister, that's why."

"Marcy?"

Ken nodded. "Did you ever hear of anything so crazy?"

Lila groped behind her for a chair and sat down weakly. She gasped, "You mean Steve—won't go, because he doesn't want to leave Marcy?"

"That's the deal," Ken said dourly. He locked his arms across his chest and sat staring off into space. Steve might not think he'd scuttled everything, but that, in Ken's estimation, was exactly what he had done. All their plans, all their figuring, of what purpose now, with Steve backing out? It wasn't as if you could take a trip like that with just anybody. Two guys, off alone for days, weeks on end—well, they had to be super-congenial. Otherwise, it was just no good. Like being shipwrecked together on a desert island—the wrong people could drive each other nuts. But he and Steve—why, it was the perfect set-up. Or it would have been, Ken reminded himself glumly, if it wasn't for this unreasonable, stupid idea of Steve's that he wasn't going to go.

And on account of Marcy, of all people! That was the pay-off!

In a way, he supposed, it served him right, him and his bright idea of pulling strings and bringing Marcy and Steve together in the first place. If he'd just kept his big hands off, chances were he wouldn't be faced with this problem now. But he'd felt sorry for Marcy, so unsure of herself where boys were concerned, unwilling to admit, even in her heart, her natural liking for Steve. His own part in it all had been as easy as two-and-two. A word dropped here, a suggestion there, and boom!—it was a big romance.

That was the trouble. It was a bigger romance than Ken had had any idea of starting. All he'd had in mind was to build up Marcy's self-confidence to the point where she'd ask Steve to take her to that dance she was mooning over, maybe have a few dates with him after that. Instead, in just a few short months, things had progressed to the point where it was practically impossible to pry Steve and Marcy apart. When Steve wasn't around, Marcy played dreamy music on the record-player and waited for the phone to ring. And when Steve called up, they'd talk for half an hour at a time. The darnedest drivel, too—enough to make you sick at your stomach.

Even when Ken and Steve got off to themselves, things weren't the way they used to be. Marcy's influence had proved disastrous to Steve's table-tennis game. He couldn't stay away from her long enough to keep properly in practice. Worse still, he wanted to talk about her most of the time. And Ken knew darned well she wasn't really half so wonderful as poor ol' Steve imagined. But loyalty kept him silent. After all, you couldn't tell a guy, even your best friend, that your sister wrapped her hair up on pieces of stockings at night to make it curly. And you had to agree tactfully, when pressed, that she looked a little like whatever movie star he was bent on comparing her with. As for confiding in him how she'd dawdle over a bubble bath, or hang onto the telephone out of sheer perversity when you had an important call to make, or how she had no more ethics than to swipe your last pair of jeans if all her own happened to be dirty—no, a brother's lips were sealed.

Ken became vaguely aware that someone was speaking to him, realized it was his mother, and came back to the present with a jolt.

"You mean," Lila was asking, "that Steve's afraid Marcy wouldn't be willing for him to go away, that she'd be angry?"

When Ken had finished explaining, in uncomplimentary detail, Steve's feelings on the subject, Lila said slowly, "I certainly didn't realize Marcy's charms were so potent as all that."

"Potent!" Ken made a snorting noise. "Ol' Steve should know he's the first guy she ever got her hooks into—the only one!"

"But you wouldn't tell him that?"

"What do you think I am?" Ken demanded with dignity.

"Maybe he'll change his mind when he's had time to think it over," Lila tried to offer some consolation. "Or can you get some other boy to go with you?"

Ken sighed. "Skip it, Mom. You don't understand."

An approaching murmur of voices came through the open windows. Lila glanced up to see Marcy and Steve walking slowly up the flagstone path from the street. Marcy's shining dark head reached barely to Steve's broad shoulder. Their glances were raptly intent on each other, their hands locked together. They were sweet.

Apparently Ken did not find them so. He leaped to his feet and streaked for the stairs. "Yipes!" he said. "I can't take it!" He warned in a hissing whisper from the landing, "Don't mention what I've been telling you, Mom. Steve doesn't want Marce to know why he isn't going with me. He's scared it might go to her head."

"Don't worry," Lila answered. She had long since learned that the best way to deal with a pair of teen-age offspring was to let them settle their own affairs insofar as was possible. Besides, she realized, unless dinner was going to consist solely of lemon cream pie, she'd have to get out to the kitchen and do something about it.

When Marcy and Steve came in a moment later, the pleasant living-room was quite deserted.

"Hi, Mom," Marcy called. "I'm home."

Her mother acknowledged this interesting bit of information from the kitchen, above a business-like clatter of pots and pans.

"Steve's here, too," Marcy announced. "May we have a Coke?"

"Of course," her mother called.

Marcy went out to the kitchen, turning on the radio as she passed it, and Steve flopped on the couch. Soon she was back, with two ice-cold bottles, each with a straw thrust into it.

"Gee, thanks," Steve said, as she sat down beside him.

They sat there, sipping their drinks and looking at each other. Steve's glance was questioning, Marcy's aloof, just a little hurt and accusing.

"You mad?" Steve asked.

Marcy shook her head. "Why should I be mad? I merely asked you a simple question. If you don't care enough about me to answer it—" she shrugged her bare tanned shoulders above the ruffled top of her green sundress.

"But I do, Marce," Steve said. "It's just—well, the name of our club's a secret. Ken and the other guys'd murder me if they found out I told you what the letters stand for."

Marcy's brows lifted. "I see. You don't trust me."

"Sure I do," Steve gulped.

"Then why do you assume I couldn't keep your secret?"

"It's not that," Steve said miserably. He finished off his Coke to the noisy end and set the bottle carefully on the floor, so as not to make a ring on the furniture.

Marcy nodded, her eyes downcast toward the remains of her own drink, her face a little sad. "You just don't like me enough, then."

All summer she had been trying to worm out of Steve the meaning of the cryptic letters that comprised the name of the club to which all the boys in the crowd belonged. And all summer he had held out against her curiosity. But today a strange forewarning that he might be about to weaken flashed its message through Marcy's mind. If she could just needle him a tiny bit further, without making him angry—

"No," Steve said in a strangled tone, reaching for her fingers. Marcy let them linger briefly in his hand, then withdrew them. "Gee, Marce, you make it tough!"

Marcy sighed, a mere little breath of sound. "Okay, Steve. I won't ask any more. I just thought—when two people like each other a lot, they should have confidence in each other—but—"

Steve looked around a shade wildly, checking on the fact that they were completely alone. The music pouring from the radio almost covered the sound of his voice, so that Marcy had to lean a little closer to hear him. "You promise you'll never tell Ken I told you, or even hint that you know?"

"Oh, yes," Marcy said solemnly, her eyes wide on his.

"Okay, then," Steve plunged, his voice going all the way down to a whisper. "It's Boys' Benevolent Protective Association For Better Understanding Between Sexes. Now are you satisfied?"

He looked so unhappy, Marcy felt a qualm of guilt at having won out. But not a very large qualm. And it was almost immediately absorbed in a delicious sense of power that poured over her in a warm tide. She felt, momentarily, like all the deathless charmers of history, who had wound men around their little fingers. Cleopatra, Delilah, Helen of Troy—Marcy drew a deep thrilled breath and smiled at Steve, a tender, grateful little smile. She reached out and curled her fingers in his beguilingly.

"Thank you, Steve," she said. He opened his mouth to speak, but she forestalled him quickly. "And I promise you I won't breathe a word about it to a soul—not Liz, not anyone. And I won't act as if I know anything about it in front of Ken."

"You better not," Steve said darkly. "I feel like a traitor."

"Don't," Marcy begged him. "We'll never speak of it again. But I want you to know it's the very sweetest thing you ever did for me, trusting me with a secret like that." She meant it, too. How could she doubt the depth of his feelings, the strength of her influence over him, after such an act of trust?

As his hand closed harder around hers, Marcy gave him a look that was absolutely dazzling. . . .

Upstairs, Ken had flopped across his bed and thumbed disinterestedly through an aviation magazine. Music smote his ears—Marcy always switched on the radio automatically when she came in. Mingled with the music were Marcy's and Steve's voices, their words quite indistinguishable. Ken thought: Yat-ta-ta, yah-ta-ta, all the time.

He turned over on his back and shut his eyes, trying to dismiss all thought of his sister and his friend. He pictured himself biking through a stretch of gorgeous scenery, vaguely reminiscent of Western movies he had seen, only dotted with pines. But he couldn't bike alone. There must be someone other than Steve who would be fun to take a trip with. Ken considered several friends without enthusiasm. Finally his thoughts hovered over Bix Meyers.

Bix was a good enough egg. They got along pretty well

together. Not so well as Steve and he, of course, Ken reflected; still Bix might fill the bill. He was agreeable and had a good sense of humor. And he was unattached, at least, temporarily. Of course, it was only a matter of time till some girl got him sewed up again. Bix was definitely the type girls went for, even aside from the fact that he had a convertible. Ken snorted derisively at the line his thoughts had taken. He asked himself: What am I figuring on, somebody to take a trip with, or the answer to a maiden's prayer— What do I care how attractive Bix is to women?

Suddenly the solution to his problem broke in Ken's mind with the effect of a skyrocket exploding in a shower of sparks. How dumb could a guy be, he wondered. Here he was, beating his brains, trying to convince himself he'd just as soon go with Bix as with Steve. But why not try to get Marcy interested in Bix? Then all his troubles would be over.

It shouldn't be too hard to accomplish, either, not for an old experienced string-puller like himself. Certainly Bix was as good-looking as Steve, he had a smoother line— and the convertible. Besides, as he'd told Marcy before, it wasn't a good thing for a girl to concentrate too exclusively on one guy.

Ken's conscience stirred just a little as he considered the effect a switch in Marcy's affections might have on Steve. But he'd get over it, just as he, Ken, was gradually getting over his disillusionment with Devon. A long leisurely vacation in congenial company would be good for them both. They could completely forget women and all kindred distractions. Of course, Ken soothed his conscience, if Steve and Marcy wanted to get together again later on, that would be okay with him. It wasn't that he wanted to bust them up permanently. He only wanted to borrow Steve for a while.

Abruptly he felt better, much better. The hard lump of his disappointment in Steve dissolved. Ken jumped off the bed, scuffing up the scatter rug in his hurry.

"Hi, you lucky people," he hailed Marcy and Steve cheerfully as he loped down the stairs, "here I come!"

Overhearing him from the kitchen, Lila reflected on the wonderful resiliency of youth. She was glad Ken had decided to make the best of things.

Chapter Thirteen

KEN PULLS A FEW STRINGS

Ken proceeded to plot his campaign carefully. The thing was, he had to work faster than he liked. If he couldn't get Steve into a frame of mind to go with him soon, it would be too late. Mid-September and the start of school was only a month off. So he didn't have much time to fool around.

Ken knew Bix and his healthy ego well enough to realize that his interest would be snared by the dropping of a few not too subtle hints that Marcy secretly thought him pretty terrific. Maybe she did, at that, Ken argued with the sense of guilt that persisted in prodding him. After all, he'd used these same tactics in getting her and Steve interested in each other and look how well that had turned out. For them, that is. Not for him.

At first Bix seemed doubtful. "She always acts like she

can't see anybody but Steve Judson."

"Oh, well," Ken discounted that, "she's used to Steve, that's the thing. They kind of take each other for granted. Besides," he lowered his tone confidentially, "I imagine she figures you're pretty much out of her league. I mean, she's just a kid."

"She's a darned cute one, though," Bix admitted, a gleam of interest brightening his gaze.

Ken observed the gleam with satisfaction. . . .

The very next day Ken came in from mowing the lawn to find Marcy just turning away from the telephone. There was a dreamy thoughtful expression on her face as she announced, "That was Bix Meyers. He hasn't called up in a long time."

"Can you blame him?" Ken asked.

"What do you mean?"

"Oh," Ken shrugged, "the way you let Steve get away with acting as if he owns you, naturally it discourages competition. It's a wonder anybody else ever bothers with you."

Marcy said, a little reminiscent smile curving her mouth, "Bix has *quite* a line, hasn't he?"

"He seldom wastes it on me," Ken admitted drily. "But I understand his date-rating's pretty high. Most girls would fall all over themselves for a chance to go out with him."

"I know they think he's smooth," Marcy agreed. "I guess he is, really. He seems—sort of older than some of the other boys."

"What did he call about?" Ken asked.

"Oh, he asked me to go to the movies tonight," there was a small, but justifiable note of pride in Marcy's voice.

"No foolin'?" Ken said admiringly. "Somehow you never just struck me as the type that would appeal to Bix. You seem—sort of kiddish for him."

"I am not!" Marcy denied hotly. "And I've gone out with Bix Meyers before. You make it sound as if I ought to be grateful to him for noticing me or something!"

"That's right," Ken said thoughtfully, "you did go out with Bix a few times. I'd forgotten. He didn't stay interested very long."

"*He* didn't?" Marcy exclaimed, indignant. "I didn't encourage him, that was all. Any more than I did today."

"You mean," Ken asked incredulously, "you're not going to the movies with him? Why?"

"Well," Marcy said slowly, "I couldn't tonight. Steve's coming over."

Ken sniffed. "Of all the dumb dames! Turning down a real honest-to-goodness date with Bix for maybe a walk and a Coke with Steve. You got a hole in your head or something?"

He sounded so serious, Marcy stared at him doubtfully. "Bix said he'd try again," she told him.

"I wouldn't count on it," Ken said drily, "a popular guy like Bix. He doesn't have to beg a girl for a date, you know."

Marcy said, "But I couldn't stand Steve up. I'd already told him I'd be home tonight," she added, in an even more doubtful tone than before. "Not that I'm so sure I'd have gone out with Bix anyway."

"Why not?" Ken demanded.

"Well—I just happen to like Steve better."

"Look, Marce," Ken said in his best big-brother-giving-advice manner. "You've got to use a little sense. Don't let any guy get the idea he owns you. Sure, Steve's a good egg and my best friend. But you're my sister and I wouldn't be doing right by you if I didn't set you straight on this. Fellas are all alike to some extent, Marce. If they get a notion a girl's just sitting home, waiting for them to show up—well, then they begin to wonder why she hasn't any other dates. They ask themselves why nobody else seems to find her as terrific as they do. You see what I mean?"

Marcy's brown eyes were steady, questioning on his. "Has Steve ever told you he feels that way?"

"No," Ken denied hastily, "he's never said a word about it. I'm only telling you how most guys feel."

Marcy brooded over the whole thing a long moment.

Then she asked, "You honestly feel a little competition's a good idea?"

Ken patted her shoulder. "You catch on fast," he said. And left it at that.

Marcy talked the matter over again later that afternoon with Liz and Rosemary. The three of them sat in a booth at the drugstore, sipping chocolate malteds and enjoying the air conditioning which turned the dim place into a cave of coolness. Outside in the street the summer sun beat down pitilessly and people could be seen going past the big window mopping their perspiring brows.

When Marcy had passed along to the two other girls, as a good friend should, the interesting fact that Bix had asked her for a date and that Ken had thought her loopy for not accepting, along with a full recounting of his reasons for this opinion, Rosemary said a shade wistfully, "I wish he practiced what he preaches."

"How do you mean?" Marcy asked.

"Well, look at me," Rosemary said. "I've been going out with Don and Hank and the rest, ever since Ken went off the deep end over Devon. And where has it got me? Exactly nowhere, so far as Ken's concerned. I don't think he's even noticed."

"Oh, sure, he has," Marcy consoled her. "It's just taking him a while to get over Devon, that's all."

"I'm sorry," Liz said, "to have such a louse for a cousin. But as for this theory of Ken's," she regarded Marcy solemnly, "I think he's absolutely right. I've found that all the boys appreciate me more when I don't concentrate too hard on any one of them. It's more fun, too."

"I don't know," Marcy said uncertainly.

"Why," Liz argued, "Bill and I were getting into an awful rut, till I turned up missing a few times when he dropped in without warning. When he realized other people saw something in me, too, he stopped taking me for granted in a hurry."

"Steve does sort of take me for granted, I guess," Marcy had to admit. "I mean, every now and then he just stops by without bothering to call up first and ask me for a date."

"I wish," Rosemary sighed, "your brother would take me for granted again. Sometimes a rut's a nice cozy place to be in."

"Don't listen to her," Liz said. "If she hadn't let Ken know he was the only one she cared a darn about, he might have stayed interested longer."

"Is that so?" Rosemary said a shade resentfully. "Can I help it if I'm the faithful type?"

"We're too young to be faithful," Liz argued. "Time enough for that when we get engaged."

How, Marcy wondered, was a girl to decide which course was wiser? . . .

But Ken wasn't even aware that Liz, quite innocently, was aiding and abetting him in his efforts to influence

Marcy. He took it for granted he was doing it all himself. During the days that followed, he felt exactly like a puppeteer, behind the backdrop pulling strings.

He didn't think he'd ever forget the blank look on Steve's face the night he dropped in without warning and discovered that Marcy had driven over to Clay City with Bix Meyers.

"With Bix?" Steve asked incredulously when Ken told him. "Why—I didn't know Marcy was going out with him again."

"He's been kind of working on her lately," Ken admitted. "Keeping the telephone wires hot. Asking her to go dancing, or to dinner, or a show."

"Some nerve," Steve grumbled.

"I don't suppose you can blame her," Ken said judiciously. "Bix is quite a guy."

"I don't think he's so hot."

Ken assumed a philosophic tone. "Women are all alike, I guess. Let one of 'em suspect you think she's tops and —whammo!—it goes to her head. She starts looking around for new conquests."

"I didn't think Marcy was like that." Steve sounded hurt.

"Oh, don't be too hard on her," Ken said. "She's just a kid. And Bix seems to be the type all the babes drool over."

"Yeah," Steve sighed deeply. "Yeah, I know."

"I'm pretty sure she likes you best," Ken consoled him.

"You really think so?"

"Anyway, she did," Ken said.

"Why the past tense?" Steve demanded.

"Well—" Ken kept his voice carefully detached, as though the question under discussion made no difference to him one way or the other, "it's just that a girl—any girl—is pretty apt to kind of grind a guy down, once she's sure she's got him where she wants him."

"Marcy?" Steve asked incredulously.

"She's a female, isn't she?" Ken pointed out. "Even if she is my sister. And females are pretty much alike, once they get the upper hand with a guy."

"Yeah, but, gee—" Steve began.

Ken interrupted, still in that confidential tone, "Personally, I think you were foolish not to figure on taking that bike trip as we planned. I mean, giving up everything for a dame—well, there's no percentage in it. She gets the idea she's too important to you. And it's a big mistake ever to let 'em realize that."

"But you promised not to tell her why I wasn't going."

"I didn't," Ken assured him. "But Marcy's smart enough to put two and two together. Why else would you decide not to go when you were so keen on the idea before you started taking her out?"

"Yeah, I guess it was kind of obvious," Steve admitted glumly.

"If you went away for a few weeks, gave her a chance to miss you, she'd probably fall all over you when you got back."

"You think so?" Steve asked wistfully. After a long interval of silence, he inquired, "You still figuring on going?"

Ken nodded. "Only for a couple of weeks, though. Haven't got too much time left till school starts."

More silence, obviously thought-filled on Steve's part. Then, "Got somebody else lined up to go with you, I suppose?"

"I've got some possibilities," Ken shaded the truth. "Haven't quite decided yet for sure."

"When you planning to get under way?"

"In about a week."

"It'll be a sharp trip all right," Steve said. He hesitated a moment. "Uh—Ken. I'm still not absolutely positive I won't go."

"You're not?" Ken's brows lifted in apparent surprise. "I thought you turned me down flat."

"Well, I guess I did. But so long as you haven't decided definitely on who to take—would you mind not making the final arrangements with anybody else till I think it over a little more?"

"If you think fast," Ken warned him. "Time's a-wastin'."

"I will," Steve grinned feebly. Then his jaw set grimly. "I don't want any girl to get the idea she can push me around too much. I'll—I'll see, Ken. I'll let you know soon."

Chapter Fourteen

STRINGS CAN TRIP

Marcy had such a good time seeing a stage show and having supper afterward with Bix in Clay City that it seemed too ungrateful to decline when he asked her to go to a movie a few nights later. It would look, she told herself, as if she only went out with him when he offered expensive plans for the evening. And this wasn't the case at all. Bix was attractive enough, amusing enough, to make even a Coke date fun. And besides, Steve hadn't been paying enough attention to her lately. He took her for granted, just as Ken had hinted, and as Liz had agreed was the case. Well, she'd show him!

So Marcy went to the early movie with Bix and afterward they had a soda and went for a ride, a short one, since Mom had made it quite clear before they left that

Marcy was to be home by ten-thirty. It was only shortly aften ten when the convertible pulled up in front of the Rhodes house. Marcy and Bix talked for not more than fifteen minutes in the car, then Bix walked her solicitously up to the front porch and they stood talking for just a couple of minutes longer. Not more than five anyway.

But no sooner had Bix driven off in the convertible and Marcy had turned to let herself into the house when a voice from the darkness almost scared her out of seven years' growth. Then she realized that it was Steve's voice and righteous anger took the place of fear.

"Steve Judson!" Marcy exclaimed furiously, feeling the hot color flood up into her face. "What are you doing, slinking around people's houses in the dark, spying on them?"

"Who's slinking?" Steve asked. "I was just sitting here on the porch, minding my own business—"

"But it's our porch," Marcy reminded him icily. "You can just mind your business elsewhere! There's nothing lower than eavesdropping, nothing in this world!"

"I wasn't eavesdropping," Steve denied. "How was I to know old smoothie Bix would bring you right up to the door? Why couldn't he let you come up the steps alone?"

"Because he's a gentleman, that's why," Marcy said.

"He sounded more like a wolf to me."

"Oh!" Marcy exclaimed. "You did listen! Steve Judson, you make me so mad I could—I could—"

"Spit?" Steve asked maddeningly.

"Now you're being vulgar," Marcy said. "But I suppose I should expect that of anyone who'd sink so low as to snoop around people's houses, waiting for them to get home so he could spy on them and listen in on their private conversations with other people!"

"I wish you'd quit saying that," there was anger in Steve's tone now, too. "All I did was come over to see you. I kind of peeked in the window and you didn't seem to be home. So I just sat down on the porch and waited for you. And then when you and Dream-boat pulled up out in front—well, I was trapped. I couldn't leave without both of you seeing me—"

"So you preferred to stay out of sight and just scare me to death, is that it?"

"I didn't mean to scare you."

"I suppose you just thought I'd welcome you with open arms."

"Well, I didn't think you'd bawl heck out of me, if you must know," Steve told her. "What's got into you, Marce?"

"Into me?" Marcy repeated. "You're the one that's acting crazy. If you wanted to see me tonight, why didn't you call up?"

"Well—you never used to mind my just—sort of—dropping over."

"It's not very complimentary to a girl," Marcy informed him, "for a boy to think he can just drop in without warning any old time he pleases and find her waiting."

"But—"

"It implies," Marcy went on coldly, "that she's a girl no other boy would ask for a date. Or else how could you just take for granted that I'd be waiting around—"

"I'm not the one who's taking things for granted," Steve exploded. "It seems to me when a girl gets so sure she's got a guy under her thumb that she can just go off with any other guy who crooks his little finger—"

"Bix did *not* crook his finger!" Marcy corrected.

"Okay, maybe he whistled," Steve said, goaded beyond his power of endurance.

Marcy's gasp of sheer outrage was clearly audible. "Steve Judson," she gritted between her clenched teeth, "you can't talk to me that way! I won't stand for it, do you hear? You go away right now and don't you ever come back. Not ever!"

"Okay," Steve said in an equally furious voice, "that'll be a pleasure. . . ."

Ken's bed-room overhung the porch, so he couldn't help hearing a part of that quarrel. Angry voices woke him from a sound sleep and at first he thought it was Marcy quarreling with Bix and that all his finagling had been in vain. Then he recognized Steve's voice, although he was still confused as to how Marcy could be arguing with Steve when she had gone out with Bix. Before he could figure it out, a slammed door and a heavy flurry of departing footsteps served as a finale.

Ken felt so guilty he couldn't get back to sleep again for quite a while. But, he assuaged his smarting conscience, he hadn't actually done anything. Oh, sure, he had offered some unasked-for advice to both Marcy and Steve. But people didn't have to follow other people's suggestions. They were always at liberty to ignore them. . . .

Still, when Steve sought him out the next day and said he'd decided to go along on the bike trip after all, Ken felt more than ever like a puppeteer. He also felt a little like a first-class heel. But he hung on hard to the comforting thought that Marcy and Steve would probably make up and get back together again as soon as the trip was over. He'd do all he could to bring about their reconciliation, he promised himself.

As the starting date approached, plans for the bike trip crowded all else from Ken's mind. They even dimmed the disturbing memory of Devon. As for Steve, he made up in grim determination what he lacked in enthusiasm. He seemed to look upon their proposed vacation as a means to an end, rather than as an end in itself. No woman, he kept assuring Ken darkly, was going to give him the run-around as Marcy had and get away with it.

Maybe, when he was gone, she'd get enough of Bix Meyers' company to suit her. But Steve didn't sound happy about it.

"Think," Ken reminded him, "how she'll appreciate you when you get back. Women always go for rugged, independent guys who make 'em suffer. You've been too easy with her."

Steve shook his head. "She won't have anything to do with me, any more than I will with her. We're washed up for keeps. . . ."

The day before the boys' intended departure, with all their gear assembled in the Rhodes' garage and anticipation running high, something happened which made Ken wonder if maybe it didn't pay to tamper with other people's lives and push them around ruthlessly, as he had presumed to do. Maybe he'd gone too far. Maybe this was Fate's way of putting him in his place.

Ken's first suspicion that something might go wrong came when his mother, after answering the telephone and talking for a few minutes, hung up and told him in a troubled voice, "That was Ann Judson. She wants me to come over and take a look at Steve."

"Take a look at him?" Ken repeated. "Why?"

"He's got a rash," Mom said, in her best professional tone, so that you could just see her wearing a crisp white uniform and little perky cap. "His mother says his head aches, too, and she's pretty sure he has a temperature."

"Oh, fine," Ken said hollowly. "That's all we need, for Steve to come down with something." He asked then, hopefully, "Could it be hives, maybe? He's allergic to strawberries, I know."

"I don't know," Mom said doubtfully. "I told Ann I'd take a look. She's called the doctor, too, of course."

Ken moped around the house after Mom left, ridden by a vast uneasiness. But there couldn't be anything drastically wrong with Steve. He'd been fine yesterday. When the phone rang a while later, Ken raced to answer it. To his surprise it was Steve calling. As soon as Ken heard his woe-begone voice, he knew that his formless foreboding had been right, that disaster of some type had struck.

"Of all the dopey developments," Steve moaned. "Of all the gosh-awful deals! Measles, that's what I've got! And at my age, too. Why, it's not even a grown-up sort of disease. It's undignified!"

"You're sure?" Ken croaked. "If you feel well enough to be talking on the phone—"

"I'm in bed," Steve cut in, "talking on the extension. And I feel lousy. But gee, Ken, I had to let you know how sorry I am to spoil all our plans—how terrible I feel—"

Ken was feeling very low himself, almost too low to

offer much consolation. Still, he tried to cheer Steve up a little. After all, a person couldn't help getting measles. It was one of those things.

"But the trip," Steve commiserated, "all shot for you and you're not sick or anything. Or will you go by yourself, Ken," he asked, "or try to get somebody else?"

"I wouldn't go alone," Ken told him. "My folks wouldn't let me and I don't think it'd be much fun, anyway. But there is one guy I might try to get, even on this short notice."

Ken's mother's voice broke in just then on the conversation. Speaking on the Judsons' other phone, she told Ken, "You've talked enough now. Steve should rest. He's quite feverish. But he was determined to tell you how sorry he was about everything."

"Okay, Mom," Ken told her and proceeded to say good-bye to Steve and hang up quickly.

"Who were you talking to?" Marcy's voice floated down from her room.

"Steve," Ken yelled up to her. "He's got measles."

"Measles?" Marcy repeated in a tone of utter incredulity.

But Ken didn't stay around long enough to enlighten her further. He yelled on his way to the door, "Mom's over there. She'll give you the gory details when she gets home. Gotta go now."

All the way to Bix Meyers' house, Ken kept admonishing himself, "Don't get your hopes up, boy. Don't count on him." But he couldn't help feeling there was a pretty good chance—

He found Bix in the garage, squatting on his heels, fussing over one of the convertible's rear tires. Still panting from his fast pace, Ken proceeded to go straight to the point. He spilled the sad tale of what had happened to ol' Steve, explained how his unexpected illness had thrown a monkey-wrench into the plans for their bike trip. He finished hopefully, "Golly, Bix, it's a super-deal—I hate to give it up. How about you coming along with me in Steve's place? Wouldn't you like to?"

"Gee, Ken," Bix tilted his blond head thoughtfully, "it sounds great. But—when you planning to leave, tomorrow?"

Ken nodded. "I know it's short notice, but Steve just got sick today. He's got all his gear and everything, I'm sure he'd let you use it. We were going to stop at hostels, it wouldn't cost much. Don't you think you could talk your folks into letting you go?"

Bix said, "I don't think they'd care. It's not that. And—gee, Ken, I think it's swell of you to ask me. I—I'd even like to go in a way. But—" he shook his head regretfully. "I just couldn't do it, that's all."

Ken stood there, staring at him, feeling sunk. "Why not?"

Bix scratched at the tire with an oil-stained finger. "I

just couldn't," he repeated. "I got too many things lined up. Dates and—well, stuff like that."

Dates? The word went echoing crazily through Ken's mind. "You mean," he croaked, "with Marcy?"

"Well, yeah, some of 'em," Bix admitted. "Most of 'em, in fact. There's the beach picnic this week-end—I asked her to that. And a week from Saturday I'm taking her to Rosemary's party."

Ken let out the breath he'd been holding so hopefully. A puppeteer, he had just discovered, could get all tangled up in his own puppet-strings! Marcy—Bix had dates lined up with her. That was why he couldn't go on a bike trip with Marcy's brother. Marcy's smart brother, who figured out the angles, and worked things psychologically—and who'd have been better off if he'd never tried to pull any strings at all.

Probably, Ken told himself wryly, if he'd asked Bix to go with him in the first place, right after he discovered Steve had cooled off on the idea of the trip, Bix would have agreed. But no, he hadn't had sense to let well enough alone, he'd had to try to manipulate the situation with his big clumsy hands, get Steve and Marcy fighting, get Bix interested in Marcy, stir things up generally.

Ken made one last desperate try. "Don't you think you could get out of your dates without making Marcy mad? I'd help you explain to her—"

He broke off. Bix was shaking his head decisively.

There was a glazed, dreamy look in his eyes, such as Ken had often noticed in Steve's eyes when the conversation happened to get around to Marcy.

Bix said positively, "Huh-uh! I wouldn't want to take any chances on getting Marcy sore. Besides, with Steve tied up in quarantine, it'll be a great chance for me to make myself really solid with her. Not," he added, "that I don't feel sorry for him and all that. But, after all, I didn't give him measles—and—well, I'd be nuts not to take advantage of a situation like that."

Ken said drearily, "Yeah. Yeah, I guess so."

"You see how it is, don't you?" Bix asked.

"Sure, I see how it is," Ken admitted. He turned away, defeated. . . .

So the bike trip was off. There wasn't anyone else he cared to ask, anyone he had a chance of persuading. There was no use banging his head against a stone wall. Somehow, looking back, it struck Ken that the whole thing had been jinxed from the start, only he hadn't been bright enough to see it. He hadn't been bright, period, Ken thought bitterly, as he turned up the flagstone walk toward home.

He went in and slumped down on the couch and thrust his long, blue-jeaned legs out before him. Marcy's voice drifted in to him from the hall. He hadn't noticed her when he came in, but it was a wonder he hadn't tripped over her. She was lying on her back on the floor, her heels on the telephone bench, as though she expected to be there for hours and hours. Unashamedly, Ken listened. She was talking to Steve in a sweetly solicitous tone—talking the most revolting drivel, as usual, enough to make a person sick at the stomach.

Ken thought: Now she's going to feel so sorry for poor ol' Steve, being sick and all, she'll probably turn around and give Bix the complete brush-off. And we'll all be right back where we started.

In a way it was funny, he supposed. Only somehow his sense of humor didn't seem to be functioning very well at the moment. At least, his silly conscience needn't trouble him any more. All his machinations hadn't accomplished anything lasting enough to feel guilty over. But the bike trip, he reminded himself. That he regretted. Losing out on that was enough to make any guy need sympathy. Now who had a good ear to pour your troubles into, who could be trusted to feel sorry?

"Hey!" Ken exclaimed suddenly. "Get off the phone, Scourge."

"Quiet, you," Marcy said. "I'm talking to Steve."

"He's not supposed to talk so much," Ken informed her. "He's got a temperature and pink spots all over him. You'll give him a relapse and then you'll be sorry. Besides," he said, "I've got an important call to make."

The fact that he still remembered Rosemary's number gave him a pleasant little glow of satisfaction.

Chapter Fifteen

OLDER MAN

By the time Steve had recovered from his siege of measles and was back in circulation once more, September was under way and the start of school uncomfortably imminent. The crowd seemed bent on winding up the summer in a whirl of activity. There were beach parties and impromptu tennis and badminton tournaments. Liz gave a party and so did Marcy and Ken. And still looming ahead—this would be after school started, of course—was the big fall dance at the country club.

"Are you going with Steve?" Liz asked Marcy one afternoon as they sat drinking limeades on the Rhodes' porch.

"Yes," Marcy said, her eyes shining with anticipation, a little smile curving her mouth. "How did you know?"

"Oh, you've been kind of nice to him since he got well," Liz said. "I just thought you'd go with him if he asked you. Besides," she added candidly, "Bix invited me, so I had a hunch you'd turned him down."

"Steve asked me first," Marcy said. "On the phone while he was still in quarantine. Are you going with Bix?"

Liz nodded.

"What about Bill?" Marcy asked.

Liz shrugged. "He didn't get around to asking soon enough. Maybe this'll teach him a lesson."

They laughed then, not over anything particularly funny. But it was nice to be young, sitting in the cool shade sipping iced drinks, knowing themselves sufficiently admired to have been invited to the fall dance by two men apiece. Life seemed wonderfully satisfying and quite uncomplicated at the moment.

Marcy said, "Ken's taking Rosemary."

"I'm glad," Liz said. "It'll be fun. The whole crowd'll be there." She asked then, as one or the other of them was bound to ask sooner or later, "What will you wear?"

Marcy frowned faintly. "I'll have to get a new formal. I've worn that old white rag Gran sent me ages ago to simply everything! Besides it's so babyish!"

"You don't have to convince me, pet," Liz soothed. "Save it for your parents."

"Mom understands," Marcy told her. "Dad's a little

more difficult. He pinned me down so I had to admit I'd only worn the white dress three times." She sighed. "But I think Mom's helping me work on him. He's softening up a little."

"It's just the other way 'round at our house," Liz said. "I can get anything I want out of my father, but Mom I have to really work on. Sometimes I think it's a disadvantage that mothers are women, too—they can see through you so easily."

"Dad isn't usually unreasonable," Marcy said loyally. "But his disposition's been a little soured lately because he's having trouble at the office."

"What kind of trouble?" Liz asked, with only the most casual interest.

"Oh, he's had to break in a couple of new assistant sales-managers in the last couple of years. And no sooner does he get them to the point where they're some help to him than the company puts them in charge of some branch office and Dad's stuck with a new man. They've just taken Henry Wilkes away from him, transferred him to Cleveland, and now Dad's starting in with a new man they've sent from Chicago to take Mr. Wilkes' place."

"Oh," Liz said. "What color dress you thinking of getting, Marcy?"

"I don't know yet," Marcy said. "Do you?"

"I've just about decided on black. Of course, I'll have

to work my parents around to seeing it my way. They think black's too old for me. But it'd be super with my hair, I think."

"It would," Marcy agreed. "Not for me, though. I'm too dark for black. I think I'll just wait to make up my mind till I see what they've got in the stores. Mom and I are going shopping tomorrow for some new school things for me—I'll look then."

"School," Liz groaned.

Marcy groaned, too, although actually she wasn't nearly so appalled at the thought of getting back to classes as custom demanded that she make out.

A few mornings later, on Saturday, Marcy and her mother and father were sitting at the breakfast table. Ken had already left for his job at the Market, but George Rhodes didn't have to go to the plant on Saturday. So he and Lila were lingering over their coffee and Marcy was taking her time with the last piece of coffee cake. Bright sunlight spilled in through the east windows, falling warmly across Marcy's neck. A little breeze ruffled the organdy curtains and turned up a corner of the paper George Rhodes was scanning casually. Everything seemed as usual. There was no way of knowing that something quite out of the ordinary was about to happen.

Marcy had just about decided that, everything being so serene, this might be a good time to broach to her father the fact that she had set her heart on a yellow taffeta formal down at the Teen Shop. But before she could open her mouth to mention this interesting fact, her father folded his paper, laid it to one side and frowned thoughtfully in Mom's direction.

"You know, Lila," he remarked in a tentative sort of tone, "I was just thinking of something."

Mom said a trifle absently, "Yes? What, dear?"

"That new assistant of mine," began Dad. "I feel sorry for him."

"I thought it was yourself you were feeling sorry for," Mom said. "This makes three assistants, doesn't it, in two years? And you found Henry Wilkes so satisfactory."

"Yes, but this new fellow—Bonner's his name, Jerry Bonner—he's a good man, too. He seems to have all Wilkes' soundness and dependability, plus a lot of fresh ideas of his own. Of course, he's only been here a little over a week, but I'm sure he's going to work out fine."

"Then why are you feeling sorry for him?" Mom asked.

"Oh, it has nothing to do with business," Dad explained. "But he's staying at the hotel till he has time to look around for an apartment."

"Oh?" Mom said, obviously still not grasping just what Dad was getting at.

"The hotel," Dad repeated, as though that ought to make everything clear. "You know, Lila, what the Westfield House is like. Why it didn't close its doors years ago is a mystery to me. The beds—" his voice broke off as though words failed him at the awful thought of them. "For that matter," he went on finally when no one else said anything, "it's enough to give a stranger a bad impression of the whole town, having to live in that—dump!"

Mom nodded. "I know. It is pretty bad."

"Bonner's already showing signs of wear and tear," Dad said. "His work's bound to suffer if he doesn't get out pretty quick. And apartments aren't easy to find."

Mom's glance, Marcy noted, was fixed contemplatively on his face. "Would you—" Mom felt her way carefully, "care to ask him here to stay for a while, George? Just till he has time to look around and find a place of his own?"

"Here?" Dad's brows rose in a look of surprise almost too perfect to be real. "Now that might be an idea. Why didn't I think of that, I wonder?"

"We have plenty of room," Mom said.

"Ye-es," Dad rubbed his chin thoughtfully, "we have, at that. You're sure it wouldn't make too much extra work for you?"

"Oh, no," Mom said. "I don't mind. I wouldn't fuss any. But it would certainly be a lot more pleasant for him than that old hotel. Why don't you ask him, George?"

"You know," Dad beamed at her, "I believe I will. I'm

certainly glad you thought of it."

Marcy yawned. Mom was really wonderful, she reflected. Now Dad would imagine he had been very subtle about the whole business, he'd think Mom would feel she'd thought of the entire idea herself. Marcy ate the last bite of her coffee cake and licked her finger tips surreptitiously, so as not to waste a single delicious buttery crumb. A fleeting thought occurred to her—not likely, of course; nevertheless the matter should most certainly be inquired into.

She asked, "Is he old?"

Her father grinned at her. "Old? I suppose you'd consider him so. Matter of fact, he's just a youngster."

Marcy was not convinced. Her father sometimes called doddering ancients of thirty-five youngsters. You never could tell.

She asked specifically, "How old?"

Her father chuckled. "What is this, a third-degree? I'm sure his full record's on file in the Chicago personnel office. I didn't ask his age, because I had no idea how vitally important it was. But I should say, off-hand, twenty-seven, twenty-eight, somewhere around that."

Pretty old, Marcy thought, but not impossibly so. Still, it wouldn't do to appear too interested, not unless she wanted to let herself in for a lot of kidding. "What's he like?" she asked casually, studying the pattern on her plate as though it really interested her.

George Rhodes winked at his wife and answered solemnly, "Why, he has the best record of any salesman in the Chicago office, Marcy. That's why the company sent him here to the main plant to help me. It's a step up for him, may lead to a branch managership, although not—Heaven willing!—till I've got some good out of him as an assistant."

"I mean," Marcy said gently, but firmly, "what does he look like? Does he resemble a human being, or does he spout statistics and sales trends and things like Mr. Wilkes did? Is he dark, or light? Does he wear glasses? Is he—"

"Take it easy," Dad broke in, laughing. "Since he's coming here to stay a while—or, at least, I suppose he'll jump at the chance—why don't you wait and check up for yourself?"

That, Marcy supposed, without feeling very excited about the whole matter, would be best. . . .

Going uptown on an errand for her mother later that morning, Marcy ran into Rosemary just outside the drugstore. Rosemary exclaimed in her usual exuberant manner, "Darling, I'm perishing with thirst. Have a Coke on me."

"Don't mind if I do," Marcy agreed and they went into the cool dimness of the drugstore together.

Over their drinks in one of the red-leather-upholstered

booths, Marcy told Rosemary, purely by way of making conversation, about her father's new assistant coming to stay with them for a while.

Rosemary's blue eyes widened in sharp interest. "You mean that fellow from Chicago, Bonning or something like that?"

Marcy nodded. "Bonner, I think it is. Why, do you know him?"

Rosemary sighed gustily, "Wish I did. My sister was telling me about him. He sounds sensational!"

Marcy remembered that Rosemary's older sister, Peggy, was employed as a secretary at the plant. Purely by accident, she had stumbled on a well of information about this new assistant of her father's. "Tell me what she said about him," Marcy demanded. "I asked my father what he was like, but you know fathers."

Rosemary nodded. "I sure do. Well, it's this way, pet. Every girl who works at the plant is dewy-eyed over him. The pop of breaking hearts can be heard for miles around."

Marcy stopped sipping her drink, the better to listen. Her eyes were intent on Rosemary's animated face.

"Peg says she thinks it's his aloof manner that does it. She believes that's the whole secret of his power, that utterly fascinating, slightly melancholy, my-good-girl-what-do-I-care-for-your-suffering attitude. As though,

Peg says, he'd as soon bash you in the face as look at you. The tender brute—sort of like Montgomery Clift, I gather."

"Wow!" Marcy said feelingly.

"Some people," Rosemary wagged her blond head, "have all the luck. Imagine living under the same roof with such a creature—and Ken, too," she added wistfully. "How long is Bonner going to stay?"

"Just till he finds an apartment."

"That's not so easy," Rosemary said.

"Yes, I know," Marcy agreed, beaming. . . .

When she got home, she learned that her father had phoned Jerry Bonner and that he had accepted with gratitude their offer to put him up. He would be there, bag and baggage, by dinner-time.

Marcy proceeded to spend the greater part of the afternoon shampooing and setting her hair, doing over her nails, and luxuriating for a dreaming timeless period in a fragrant bubble bath. A sense of keen anticipation, an awareness of something wonderful and different about to happen, lifted her spirits. She sang as she moved about her room, gathering up her clothes. The phone rang and Mom answered it, then called upstairs, "For you, Marcy. It's Steve."

"Oh—Steve," Marcy said, as if for a moment she couldn't quite remember who Steve was. "Well—just a minute. I'll be there."

She padded down the stairs in her bare feet, her white terry-cloth robe knotted tightly around her slim waist. "Steve?" she said. "Hi."

"Hi, yourself," Steve told her. "I tried to call you earlier, but your mother said you'd gone uptown."

"Yes, I did," Marcy admitted. "I've been awfully busy."

"Doing what?" Steve asked conversationally.

"Oh, things," Marcy said. "I'm still quite rushed. Did you—was there anything special you called about?"

"In short, get to the point—huh?" Steve chuckled. "Well, yes, as a matter of fact there was something special. I wanted to invite you to drive over to Clay City with me tonight. Dad says I can have the car, so I thought we could see a stage show and—"

"Oh, dear," Marcy said in a tone of polite regret, "I'm sorry, Steve. But I can't possibly tonight."

"You can't?" Steve asked incredulously. "Why not? You got another date?"

"We-ell, no. No, I haven't any date. It's just—well, there's a business associate of my father's who's coming for dinner. He's going to stay here with us for a while."

"Live with you, you mean?" Steve asked.

"Just till he finds a place of his own," Marcy said.

"But—" Steve groped, "I don't get it. Even if your folks are having company, can't they entertain him? Why can't you go—"

"No," Marcy said firmly. "I'm sorry, Steve. But it—well, it's just out of the question. I couldn't be so rude as to simply go off with you the very first night Mr. Bonner's here."

"Look," Steve said, obviously striving for patience, "am I nuts, or are you? You don't figure you have to stay home when your folks have the Kendalls over, or my folks, or—"

"That's quite different," Marcy said. "Mr. Bonner is a stranger in Westfield. The least I can do is help make him welcome."

"Mr. Bonner?" Steve repeated, apparently struck by something for the first time. He asked darkly, "Where's Mrs. Bonner?"

"Oh, there isn't any," Marcy said. "Mr. Bonner is single."

After a moment, Steve asked, "How old is this guy?"

"Twenty-seven or so. Dad wasn't quite sure."

A sigh of relief from the other end of the wire brushed Marcy's ear. "Oh, well, that's okay if he's that old. But now look, Marce—"

"I'm sorry," Marcy said firmly, "but I'm going to stay home tonight. It was nice of you to ask me, Steve, but—some other time. 'Bye, now," she hung up quickly, before Steve could argue the matter further, and made her way languidly, dreamily, up the stairs.

Chapter Sixteen

THE QUARREL

Later, looking back on it all, it seemed to Marcy that the whole course of her life was altered the night Jerry Bonner came to stay with them. No one else in the family, not her mother or father, certainly not Ken, seemed to feel the profound change in the very atmosphere of the house that Jerry's mere presence effected. All Marcy's senses seemed sharpened, her perceptions made more acute from the moment she met this dark, rather serious, very attractive young man. He wasn't, actually, much like Montgomery Clift at all. He was simply himself, Jerry Bonner, tall, with broad shoulders, and a rather angular face that lit with his occasional smile. Surprisingly, with his dark hair, he had very blue eyes. Maybe an Irish grandmother, Marcy suspected, and there was something rather romantic about the thought.

It was his mouth, she decided, that must have given Rosemary's sister and the other girls at the plant the idea that he was hard, unyielding. There was a firmness about it and about the set of his chin that might give that impression. Only Marcy wasn't fooled by it.

She thought dreamily, just toying with her food at dinner, so intent was she on studying Jerry Bonner. Why, he isn't hard, or brutal, or anything like that. He's been hurt, that's what. And he's trying to cover up by pretending he doesn't care, that it didn't make the slightest impression on him. But it did. He's suffered. I can tell. I'll bet it was a girl, too—something a girl did to him, some terrible disappointment he's had. . . .

"Marcy, what's the matter with you?" Mom's voice broke into her day-dreaming. "You've hardly touched your Swiss steak and it's usually your favorite food. You aren't feeling—"

"No," Marcy interrupted quickly, before Mom could embarrass her further, talking to her as though she were a child with an upset stomach, and in front of *him*, too. "No, I feel fine. It's just—well, it's such a lovely night and all—well, I just don't feel especially hungry."

"Good," Ken said, "give me her dessert then, Mom. She won't appreciate it."

Marcy let her gently supercilious glance rest on Ken's teasing face for a moment. Then she said, "Yes, do that, Mother. Growing boys need extra nourishment."

"Who's growing?" Ken demanded, pricked. "I'm not growing as much as you are. Say—" he exclaimed, his gaze brightening, "I get it! She's worried about getting fat, that's it," he informed the rest of them. "I've heard Steve say a hundred times he can't stand fat women—"

Marcy's eyes blazed. "I am not, Ken Rhodes! I haven't gained a single ounce in months. And what's more I don't care a darn what Steve—" she broke off, turning a mildly amused smile in Jerry Bonner's direction, dismissing Ken in her best woman-of-the-world manner, "Isn't he infantile?"

"Oh, brother!" Ken said. "Look who's talking!"

But Marcy didn't hear him. Jerry's blue eyes had met hers and a bond of secret understanding seemed to have been established between them with that look. It seemed to Marcy Jerry's glance said plainly, "I know how it is. I understand what you have to put up with, being the younger in actual years, and yet so much older than he in knowledge of life, in understanding. Why, in all the ways that matter, you're a woman, no matter what your age, or how inexcusably your family fail to appreciate the fact."

Aloud he said simply, "Well—I can remember how much fun I used to have teasing my sister."

"We're certainly acting as if you're one of the family, Bonner," Dad said. "This sort of thing goes on between these kids all the time. Of course, it's been quite a while since they actually came to blows."

Marcy smiled at her father sweetly, although she found his attitude quite provoking. "Now, Dad, don't talk as if we're children."

"Yes, George, for pity's sake," Mom said, in that tone Marcy was never quite sure whether to take seriously or not.

"Can't we have dessert now, Mom?" Ken asked. "Everybody's through but Marcy and she's just dawdling. Steve and I are driving over to Clay City and we want to get going early."

"Steve and you?" Mom repeated on a note of faint surprise.

"Yeah, he's got their car. He asked Marcy first, but she turned him down. I didn't have a date, either, so we thought we'd take in a stage show."

"Sounds like fun," Marcy said in a slightly condescending tone. "I'll help take off the plates, Mom. We don't want to hold the boys back from their big evening."

Later, relating the scene at the dinner table to Steve, Ken demanded, "How do you like that? She didn't even sound like herself. I don't know exactly who she was trying to imitate, but she sounded as superior as if she were ten years older than me instead of a couple of years younger. That little Squirt!"

Steve said morosely, "The whole business doesn't make

sense. She couldn't have a crush on the guy, could she? Why, he's old enough to be her father!"

"Not quite," Ken said thoughtfully. "I wonder—" After an extended silence, broken only by the hum of the tires as they drove through the quiet night toward Clay City, he exclaimed, "You know, that could be it! A crush! Now why didn't I think of that?"

"But Marcy's too old for crushes on older guys," Steve objected. "She's sixteen now, she's grown-up. Crushes are what little kids get on their camp life-guards, or a man teacher maybe."

"It could happen even at sixteen," Ken argued. "It sure has all the symptoms of something like that. Look at it calmly now. Here's Marcy, turning down a sharp date with you in order to stay home because the guy's coming to live at our house for a while. She was dressed to kill at dinner, too. I realize that now. No jeans and an old shirt of my father's tonight—no sir! Her hair was all curled and she had on a good dress. And the way she acted! You'd think she was thirty if she was a day, all those airs and graces of hers. Now I realize it must have all been for the purpose of impressing him."

"But, Holy Cow, Ken," Steve said unhappily. "Can't you do something about it? Talk to her like a Dutch uncle, make her see she's acting loopy."

Ken shook his head regretfully. "I'd like to," he said. "Certainly my sympathy is all with you. But—I made myself a resolution a little while back. I decided to keep my big nose out of other people's affairs, let 'em work their problems out for themselves. If I started in now trying to show Marcy she was making a mistake going overboard for Bonner—no, I'm sorry, Steve, but I just can't do it. Not even for you. There's one bright spot, though."

"What?" Steve asked dully.

"Marcy'll get over it fast. You wait and see. She's got good sense. I guess getting crushes is just one of those silly stages a girl has to go through sometime in her life. It caught up with Marcy a little late, that's all. She isn't quite as grown-up as we gave her credit for being. . . ."

But being patient was one thing and letting a girl walk all over you quite another, Steve decided as time passed. A guy could put up with anything for a day or two, but when the intolerable situation stretched out to a week—well, it was just too much!

"How much longer is this dead-beat going to park on your folks?" Steve demanded, walking home with Marcy after the first day of school.

"He's not a dead-beat!" Marcy flew to Jerry Bonner's defense hotly. "He's looking for an apartment all the time."

"Yeah, I'll bet." Steve kicked a dead twig out of his way viciously. "If he's so busy looking for an apartment, how's it happen he has so much time to spend at your house that you can't ever go out with me when I ask you?"

"Well—" Marcy hesitated, "for one thing he's been teaching me bridge. It's the most fascinating game, Steve. I've been playing with Jerry and Mom and Dad. Jerry's quite an expert, really."

"He's an expert all right," Steve growled, "only why can't he find somebody his own age?"

"Just what do you mean by that?" Marcy asked coolly.

"Why doesn't he take out some of the girls at the plant, if he craves female companionship? Or is he trying to save his money, sitting home teaching you bridge and sponging on your folks?"

Marcy's eyes blazed. "Steve Judson, it's absolutely none of your business who my folks invite to stay with us. Or how long he stays, either."

"Yeah, but you're my business," Steve insisted, reaching for her hand.

Marcy snatched her fingers away as though his touch burned.

She said, "You haven't a thing to say about what I do. If I want to stay home and—listen to records and play bridge and—indulge in intelligent conversation, instead of doing a lot of childish chasing around whenever you take a notion—"

"Oh," Steve said, "so now I'm childish, am I? I suppose to interest you, a guy's got to be thirty years old, with one foot in the grave!"

"That's the most ridiculous thing I ever heard of," Marcy said in her most supercilious tone. "Jerry's not thirty. And he's the most vital, the most alive person I ever met. Why, his eyes can say more to you, without one word passing his lips—"

"What," Steve broke in, "have his talking eyes said to you, may I ask? And exactly how do you know they're saying what you think they are?"

"Because I'm perceptive," Marcy explained. "I don't have to have everything drawn out and diagrammed for me, as some people seem to. For instance, he's never said a word about it, but I know Jerry Bonner's unhappy. He's suffered. I'm sure he's been in love, really deeply in love, with some girl who let him down—"

Steve snorted. "Of all the romantic drivel! It's a lot more likely he doesn't like Westfield and is sorry he came here. Probably that's all he's unhappy about, if he is unhappy and you aren't just letting your imagination work overtime. I suppose it would seem kind of dull here after Chicago, maybe even dull enough to drive a guy to taking up with little girls half his age in order to pass the time."

"Steve Judson, I'm *not* half his age! And he hasn't 'taken up with me' as you put it. We've never gone anywhere together at all—only for a couple of walks."

"Walks even!" Steve exploded. "When I take you out I spend a little money on you, anyway!"

"Are you implying that I make you spend money?" Marcy demanded furiously.

"No," Steve said, "I do it of my own accord. When I have a girl, I show her a little fun. Like the country club dance next Saturday. I asked you to that, didn't I? I'll be getting you a corsage and—"

"Maybe," Marcy said icily, "you'd rather save the money!"

"Maybe," Steve said with equal coldness, "you'd rather stay home and practice your bridge—with Jerry Bonner!"

Marcy was so furious, she felt hot tears crowding her eyelids—and that made her angrier than ever. She said, "All right, Steve Judson, if that's the way you're going to be—the nasty, mean, domineering way!—I won't go to the dance with you! I'm sorry I ever planned to. I was all through with you once before—and then you went and got measles to work on my sympathy! But I should have had more sense than to make up with you!"

"I'm the one should have had sense," Steve corrected, his gray eyes bitterly cold. "I suspected you were pretty fickle when you gave me the go-by for Bix Meyers. But now that you've got a yen for this old creep Bonner—

well, you can have him for all of me. And I won't bother you again—not ever!"

Turning on his heel he stalked off. And Marcy was so angry she couldn't even think of a last word to speed him on his way!

Chapter Seventeen

NIGHT OF THE DANCE

When Marcy told Liz about her quarrel with Steve, Liz said deploringly, "It certainly wasn't a very practical time to break up with him."

"Practical!" Marcy exclaimed, her eyes flashing. "Why, I was never so mad—"

"Yes," Liz broke in, "I know. I can imagine just how you felt. But it seems to me you might have managed things so you didn't have a big fight till after the fall dance." She shook her blond head regretfully. "Now you're left out in the cold."

"I don't care!" Marcy said fiercely. But it wasn't true. She did care about losing out on the dance at the country club. This was to have been her first time. Last year she had been too young, nobody had asked her to go. She'd been looking forward to the occasion for weeks. She had even felt confident Dad would buy her the yellow taffeta formal. But now— She informed Liz firmly, "I wouldn't go with Steve Judson if he were the last man on earth!"

Liz patted her shoulder sympathetically. "I know," she said. "And I'm not blaming you for getting mad at him. It's just—" she sighed, "Well, it seemed as if it was going to be such fun, all the crowd there together. It just isn't going to seem right, Marcy, without you and Steve."

"Quit talking about us," Marcy requested, "as though we're still a twosome."

"Okay," Liz said. "But I can be sorry, can't I? . . ."

Marcy could be sorry, too, secretly. Not that she would admit having any regrets. There was her pride to uphold her. But pride is such a stiff, unyielding companion. Sometimes Marcy couldn't help feeling just a little sorry for herself. And on one of these occasions, when she was sitting pensively on the couch, staring off into space, Ken caught her at it.

"Serves you right," Ken said a trifle gruffly, "scrapping all the time with a good guy like ol' Steve. Now you got yourself out on a limb and sawed the limb off. That wasn't very bright."

Marcy said coolly, "I can't imagine what you're talking about. Nothing is farther from my thoughts than Steve Judson. Besides," she reminded him, "weren't you the one who told me it wasn't a good idea to concentrate too exclusively on one boy?"

Ken snorted derisively. "Don't go trying to pass the buck to me now. I certainly didn't imply it was smart to ditch a fella like Steve for some middle-aged character who's only interested in you from a fatherly viewpoint."

"That," Marcy informed him, "is absurd. Jerry's not one bit fatherly."

"Well, he ought to be," Ken said. "Otherwise he's a cradle-snatcher. I don't know what Mom and Dad are thinking of, letting him hang around here, putting dopey ideas in your feeble brain till you can't think straight."

"I can so think straight," Marcy said hotly. "Just because I finally realized I was too mature for Steve Judson—"

"Too mature?" Ken chortled. "That's a laugh! Why, getting a crush on an old guy like Bonner's a sure sign of infancy."

"You—shut up!" Marcy said, stalking majestically past him toward the stairs. She had to move fast to achieve the privacy of her room and slam the door before the hot tears spilled over. . . .

As the date of the dance approached, the atmosphere around the Rhodes house grew even heavier. Not only was Marcy in a low state of mind, but Lila, too, suffered pangs of disappointment. Mother-like, she had been anticipating the gala evening vicariously. Now Marcy's quarrel with Steve had spoiled everything for both of them.

"Honestly," Lila said to her husband one evening when they were alone in their bed-room, "I think the stage Marcy's going through is just as hard on me as it is on her—and I'm not quite sure I can take it at my age."

"Oh, come now," George said. "You've felt that way about all her stages. We'll all live through this—I think." He asked then, "Just what did she and Steve have a fight about this time?"

Lila shook her head. "I'm not quite sure. Marcy's never said in so many words and I don't like to pry. But I suspect it's on account of Jerry Bonner."

"Bonner?" George's eyebrows shot up. "What's he got to do with Marcy and Steve, for Heaven's sake?"

"I think," Lila confided, "Steve's jealous of him."

"Of Bonner?" George laughed then. "Why, that's the silliest thing I ever heard of. Bonner's years too old for her."

"I know," Lila nodded. "And you know and I'm pretty sure Jerry knows—but does Marcy?"

"You mean she—has a crush on Bonner?"

Lila said dreamily, "I can remember quite well when I was in high school. I was so smitten with Professor Laird I took Algebra and Geometry, although I hated Math. And he even had a wife and two children and was beginning to get quite a high forehead. Girls are very susceptible to—shall we say mature charms?—at that age. So I don't think we ought to be too hard on Marcy."

"I'd say she's being hard on herself, losing out on a date with Steve for the fall dance, all because of a man who, I'm sure, looks on her as a mere child."

"I suppose so," Lila sighed. . . .

Dinner the Saturday night of the dance proved a rather hectic meal. Not that the food wasn't quite satisfactory. But Ken was in a rush to get into his tuxedo and Marcy's eyes were so suspiciously bright that both her parents kept glancing at her anxiously to be sure she wasn't just about to burst into tears. Jerry Bonner would have had to be blind and deaf in order not to notice the cross-currents of excitement eddying all about. And he would have had to be devoid of human curiosity not to ask a few questions.

"So the fall dance is the big affair of the season," he said, when he had managed to secure a bit of information on the subject from Lila. "Are you and Mr. Rhodes going tonight?"

George said, "Dancing is not one of my favorite pastimes, Bonner. Lila gave me up as a bad job in that department long ago. I even think she's reconciled by this time."

"Besides," Lila said, "it's mostly the young people who turn out in a big way for the dances."

Jerry Bonner nodded. All unaware of the crisis he was

precipitating, he asked Marcy and Ken, "You two are going, of course."

Ken said, "I am—but—" his uncomfortable glance brushed Marcy.

"I'm not," Marcy said quite clearly.

There was a jagged little moment of silence and then everyone, it seemed, began talking at once. Everyone, that is, except Marcy, who sat quietly, staring down at her plate. After a moment she pushed aside her partly eaten dessert and said to her mother, "I—don't think I care for any more. May I be excused?"

"Of course, dear," her mother said.

She went out of the dining-room and up the stairs and they could hear the definite sound of her bed-room door closing.

Ken pushed back his chair and got up. "Me, too. Mom. I gotta get going. I haven't had my bath yet and there's that shirt to get into and that tie to tie. Bix and Liz will be stopping by for me fairly early, then we'll go pick up Rosemary."

Lila nodded and Ken left the room. With just three of them left at the table, Jerry Bonner asked. his tone a trifle troubled, "Did I put my foot in it someway? I assure you I didn't mean to."

"We know that, Bonner," George said.

Jerry went on, "I never thought of Marcy not having a date for the dance. She's such a lovely girl. The boys around here must be crazy."

Lila smiled ruefully. "Well, she did have a date. She was going with Steve. But then—just a few days ago, they had a big quarrel."

"Marcy's obviously feeling very low tonight over the whole business," her father added.

Jerry said, "Poor kid. I'm sorry I had to be the one to rub salt in her wounds, even if I didn't mean to."

"As a matter of fact," George said, "you were the cause of their quarrel, Bonner."

Lila gave him a warning shake of the head, but it was too late. Her, "Now, George—" was swallowed up in Jerry Bonner's astonished, "I was? But how—what did I do—what—?"

"Oh, you didn't do a thing," George chuckled. "It was all in Steve's mind. But he resented you sufficiently to say too much, more than Marcy would take. So they had a scrap."

"You mean—" Jerry asked incredulously, "Steve was jealous—of me?"

Lila admitted, "That's it, Jerry—although George shouldn't have told you. After all, it wasn't your fault."

"I feel guilty just the same," Jerry said. "I suppose I have been selfish, taking up any of Marcy's time at all. I had no right to do that, I just didn't think."

"But she wanted you to teach her to play bridge," Lila pointed out.

"Yes, but even so," Jerry argued, "I shouldn't have taken any chance of making trouble for her with Steve." He regarded the glowing tip of his cigarette thoughtfully for a moment, then glanced up at Lila. "Is Steve taking another girl tonight?"

Lila shook her head. "No, Ken says he's going stag. I suppose that's just to show Marcy he doesn't care. But—"

"Look," Jerry interrupted, his eyes moving from Lila to George inquiringly, "if you two have no objection, how about me taking Marcy to the dance? I feel like such a heel, having spoiled the whole thing for her. After all, I've got a kid sister of my own, I know how she'd suffer over getting left out of all the festivities after she'd planned on going. And maybe," he went on, "when she and Steve see each other there, they'll make up. Then I can turn her over to him, and he'll realize how unfounded his suspicions of my motives were, and no harm will have been done. What do you say?"

"Why—" Lila felt her heart begin to beat a little faster, "it sounds like a fine idea to me. What do you think, George?"

Her husband chuckled. "Bonner, you must have been a Boy Scout in your youth. But if you want to do a good deed and the idea strikes Marcy as okay, who am I to object?"

It seemed to Marcy that the next hour or so passed

in an incredible rosy dream. From the moment Mom knocked on her door and said, a little breathless note in her voice, "Marcy, won't you come out? Jerry's just had a wonderful idea," a kind of fairy-tale quality pervaded the very atmosphere. Certain highlights stood out unforgettably. Ken's unbelieving face as he exclaimed, "You're going to the dance with Jerry? Golly Moses!" And there was Mom's triumphant smile as she turned from the telephone to announce, "Matt says he'll take care of it himself and have the corsage here within half an hour. Orchids, no less!" Orchids would do so much for her old white formal, Marcy thought. And, of course, the dress wouldn't seem old at all to Jerry, who had never seen it.

She felt as Cinderella must have felt, getting ready for the ball. Only Cinderella had merely been hoping to meet her prince, while Marcy was going with Jerry Bonner. When she came downstairs at last, her white dress with its silver sequins like scattered stars swirling about her, the orchid corsage in her hand, so it wouldn't be crushed by her velvet evening coat, Marcy's feet seemed scarcely to touch the stairs. And Jerry, waiting in the hall for her, had never looked so handsome as he did in dinner coat and black tie. Marcy's breath went out in a little sigh of sheer delight, as she thought of the envy with which all the girls in the crowd would regard her, the bitter blow her arrival with Jerry would be to Steve.

"You look lovely," Jerry told her, smiling his nice infrequent smile that didn't quite touch the sadness in his eyes.

So do you, Marcy thought. But aloud she said merely, "Thank you."

Her father handed Jerry the car keys. Her mother patted Marcy's shoulder and smoothed an imaginary wrinkle from her dress. And then there was the customary little flurry of "good-byes" and "have funs" and "don't be *too* lates" and Marcy and Jerry were outside in the crisp September night and the wonderful evening was acutally beginning.

Driving along, her shoulder pressing companionably against Jerry's as they went around curves, Marcy asked the question that had been nagging at her. "Will you tell me the absolute truth about something, Jerry? Did my parents—ask you to take me tonight?"

"Of course not," Jerry said definitely. "It was my idea."

"That's all I wanted to know," Marcy said relievedly. "Now let's not say another word about it. Let's just enjoy ourselves."

"That," Jerry said, "is a fine idea. . . ."

Marcy didn't think she would ever forget the look on Steve Judson's face when she came into the big country club ballroom with Jerry Bonner. Disbelief struggled with dismay, twisting his features ludicrously.

"Evidently," Jerry murmured in Marcy's ear as they

began dancing, "your brother didn't tell him we were coming."

Marcy laughed up at Jerry, pointedly ignoring Steve. "Trust Ken not to spoil a climax. He figured Steve would find out for himself soon enough."

Each familiar face that Marcy's glance encountered looked surprised. Liz, dancing with Bix, asked Marcy endless questions with her eyes. Rosemary, moving past in Ken's arms, was apparently pumping him for information. Good old Ken, Marcy thought. He had really let her startle them all with her unexpected appearance. But after a moment or two, she stopped looking around to see the effect of her arrival on her friends. Instead she concentrated her attention on Jerry Bonner.

"You dance awfully well," she told him.

"Little rusty, I'm afraid," Jerry said. "You're the one who's good." He added, after a moment, "Don't feel you have to stick with me all evening. This is your night, Marcy. I want you to really enjoy it. If Steve asks you for a dance—"

"He won't," Marcy said. "We're not speaking."

"Well—" Jerry hesitated, "if he shows signs of wanting to make up, you wouldn't just heartlessly squelch him, would you?"

Marcy shrugged. "I might," she said airily. "Just now I feel as if I don't want to be bothered."

Down inside, though, Marcy felt a glow at the realization that her appearance with Jerry had really stunned Steve. It served him right, she reflected, trying to be so smart and coming stag to the dance, just because he knew she couldn't get there without an escort. Well, she had an escort, one who seemed perfectly contented to be here with her. An older man, a smooth dancer, a stimulating conversationalist—it seemed almost too good to be true. She hadn't actually dared to hope before tonight that Jerry Bonner found her as attractive as she found him. But now she could not doubt it. And, after all, what was a mere ten years' difference in age? Marcy emerged from an exciting day-dream to the fact the music had stopped.

Bix Meyers asked her for the next dance and Jerry danced with Liz. During the intermission Liz and Rosemary cornered Marcy in the powder-room, demanding explanations.

"He's sensational," Liz said. "How'd he happen to bring you, Marcy?"

And Rosemary sighed ecstatically, "He's even more wonderful than Peggy said, you lucky thing!"

"Oh," Marcy said in a casual tone, "he is nice. As for his bringing me, it was just one of those things. As soon as he learned I wasn't coming with anyone else, he simply leaped at the chance." She powdered her nose, freshened her lipstick, as the other two girls looked on admiringly.

"I'll have to go now," Marcy said. "Jerry's waiting for me."

As a matter of fact, he was pacing up and down impatiently when Marcy joined him. He said, "I thought you'd never come."

"Why, Jerry—" Marcy's tone was faintly surprised.

"Marcy," he caught her elbow, "will you come outside on the terrace with me? I've got to talk to you, I've got to tell you something. . . ."

"Why, of course," Marcy said. And was aware of Steve Judson's lowering glance following her and Jerry through the French doors and into the romantic darkness beyond.

Chapter Eighteen

MARCY'S ADVENTURE

It was shortly after eleven when Ken felt an insistent tap on his shoulder and turned to find Steve Judson frowning beside him. "Ken, I gotta tell you something," Steve said. "It's—kind of private."

"Well, sure, Steve," Ken said. He proceeded to excuse himself from the little group with whom he had been talking, a group composed of Rosemary and Liz and Bix, whose curious glances followed Ken and Steve as they withdrew to a secluded corner.

"What's on your mind?" Ken asked.

"It's Marcy," Steve's voice was troubled. "She's gone, Ken."

"Gone?"

"I'll tell you all I know about it," Steve said, "and you can decide what to do. After all, you're her brother. I don't mind admitting I'm kind of worried."

"About Marcy?" Ken groped. "But where'd she go?"

"That," Steve's tone was portentous, "is the question. A while back, during intermission while Marcy was in the powder-room, that guy Bonner got a phone call. Don't know what it was about, he took it at a booth in the lobby, but he sure seemed excited over it. He was pacing up and down, practically biting his fingernails, when Marcy joined him. And right away quick he grabbed her by the arm and took her out on the terrace. I happened to be standing close enough to hear him say something like, 'I've gotta talk to you, gotta tell you something.' Naturally, I was a little curious, so I just sort of walked past the French doors and looked out. They were standing out there, real close together, talking awfully serious it looked like. And then pretty soon he took her arm and they went rushing down the steps to the drive and got into your folks' car and drove off. Naturally, there wasn't anything I could do, it not being any of my business or anything. But I don't trust that guy, Ken, and they've been gone way over an hour now and it seems pretty funny to me. What do you think?"

Ken grinned. "I think you've been listening to too many radio mysteries. Who do you think you are, a private eye? So Marcy went somewhere with Jerry Bonner, probably out for a hamburger."

"They've got food here," Steve reminded.

"Yeah, but maybe they didn't feel like fancy sandwiches and punch."

Steve shook his head. "He didn't act like anybody who just had a yen for a hamburger. He was worried, Ken, I'm telling you. And then his grabbing Marcy and dragging her off with him—"

"You mean she didn't go willingly?" Ken demanded.

"Oh, she seemed willing enough. But how do you know what kind of a story he handed her? Marcy's just a kid, she'd believe anything."

"So, I'm beginning to think, would you," Ken said drily.

"Yeah, but it's been so long, Ken," Steve argued.

"Look," Ken soothed, "relax, why don't you? I know her coming here with him gave you a nasty shock. Personally, I think that was her main purpose, just to shock you. But be that as it may, there's no reason for you getting into a hassle over her going out for a little drive with him. Didn't you ever leave a dance with a girl and stay an hour?"

"Well—yeah, but—"

"Okay," Ken said. "Come on now, join the rest of the gang and stop stewing. Marcy'll be back, you'll see. . . ."

But a half hour passed and she wasn't back. Now Ken was watching for her, too. And gradually a faint sense of uneasiness grew in him. Steve was fit to be tied. Naturally their mounting alarm aroused the curiosity of

Rosemary and Liz and Bix, who had by this time noted Marcy's absence. So Steve had to re-tell his story for their benefit.

"It is kind of queer," Liz said thoughtfully. She glanced at Rosemary. "You know how thrilled she was over the dance and all when we were talking to her in the powder-room. Isn't it odd she'd just—leave like that and not come back?"

"Yes," Rosemary nodded, "it is a little odd. Even if Jerry Bonner asked her to go off somewhere with him, it seems as if Marcy would have rather stayed here and danced."

"Look, you females," Ken said, "quit trying to make out as if there's something ominous about it. You trying to scare me?"

"I'm already scared," Steve admitted. "The whole business seems fishy to me."

"What do you think they've done?" Bix asked. "Eloped?"

"Eloped?" squealed Liz and Rosemary in unison.

"Are you all loopy?" Ken demanded. "Marce wouldn't do a thing like that. Neither would Bonner."

"How do you know about Bonner?" Steve asked narrowly. "Seems to me he's practically a perfect stranger. Oh, sure, he works for your Dad, but what do you actually know about him personally? He comes to Westfield and he seems okay, so your folks take him in and all—

but he could be—well, anything."

"A gangster, see," Bix said in his best Edward G. Robinson manner. "Just one of the mob, taking it on the lam, hiding out in the sticks till the big town cools off enough for him."

"Cut it out, Bix," Steve said, scowling. "This isn't any joke. You can all clown around if you like, but I think there's something queer going on, something very queer."

"Look," Ken said, laying a hand on his shoulder, "you've got me worried, too. Tell you what, Steve. I still think they're just out somewhere getting a bite to eat. Why don't you drive around to a few places, the Lighthouse and some of the drive-ins they'd be most likely to stop at? Take a look and if you don't see them, come back and let me know. How about it?"

"Well, okay," Steve said. . . .

When he got back, he looked more worried than ever. He seemed to have forgotten all about being angry at Marcy and none of the others thought to remind him of the fact. They all hovered uneasily at the edge of the dance floor, disregarding the excellent music and the other couples moving past.

"Not a sign of them," Steve said. "I tried every place I could think of, but nobody'd seen them at all."

"It's the craziest thing I ever heard of," Ken said.

And Liz added, frowning, "It's not like Marcy, not

like her a bit, just to—disappear."

"Aw, you're all a bunch of crepe-hangers," Bix grinned. "Let's face it, there are other things you can do when you slip away from a dance besides eat."

"Yeah, but not Marcy and that—that—" words failed Ken. "Why, he made out to my folks he was just taking her to the dance so she wouldn't be disappointed. And now—gee, I don't know what to do."

"You don't suppose," Rosemary said thoughtfully, "they could have gone home? Marcy didn't say anything about having a headache or anything, but—"

"Say!" Ken grabbed at the straw eagerly. "They might have done that. They just might have!"

Steve said dourly, "It doesn't sound very logical to me."

Bix asked, "Why don't you call up and find out?"

Ken shook his head. "If they weren't there, it'd scare my folks silly. No, I think Steve and I better drive home—"

"Why don't we all go?" Liz broke in. "The dance is just about over anyway. And none of us will have an easy minute now till we find out where Marcy and Jerry Bonner have gone."

Everyone favored this suggestion. They went out and piled into Bix's convertible, all but Steve, who had driven his family's car to the dance. With Steve leading the way, they covered the five miles between the country club and the Rhodes house in considerably less time than usual.

As was to be expected, the house was dark, except for the porch-light and hall-light which Mom invariably left on when any member of the family was out for the evening.

"Maybe Marcy's gone to bed," Rosemary whispered to Ken as they all tip-toed up the walk.

"I'll go in and check," Ken whispered back.

He left the others in a worried huddle on the flagstones. Crossing the porch quietly, he let himself in, then shut the door carefully behind him and mounted the carpeted stairs. He'd have sworn he didn't make a sound. But Mom's voice, low and expectant, inquired from the darkness of her and Dad's room, "Is that you, Marcy?"

"No," Ken gulped, "it's me." And then, anxiously, he asked, "Isn't Marcy home yet?"

"Why, no," Mom said, obviously surprised at his question.

"You're sure?" Ken's heart thudded against his heels.

"Why, of course. We just got to bed ourselves."

Dad's voice broke into the conversation then. "I think she's downstairs. I can hear somebody whispering under the window."

"That's the gang," Ken said miserably. "We were all

—sort of worried over Marce. So they came home with me to see if she'd got here yet."

"Ken," there was a note of alarm in Mom's voice, "why are you worried over her? What's happened?"

The bedside lamp clicked on and light fell on Mom's and Dad's anxious faces. They blinked in the sudden glare, then Mom reached for her robe on the foot of the bed, put her feet out onto the floor. "Ken, tell us!"

"Yes, for Heaven's sake!" Dad was sitting up now, too.

Ken proceeded to tell them. He had no choice. When he had finished his somewhat rambling story, he said, "Of course, it may not amount to anything. But Steve was about to have a kitten and he got us all worried."

Mom and Dad stared at each other. Mom said, "George, that wire— Do you suppose that had anything to do with it?"

"What wire?" Ken demanded.

"Western Union called here," his father explained. "Around ten-thirty it must have been. Said they had a wire for Bonner. So I told them he could be reached at the country club. That must have been the call Steve saw him get. But I don't see what connection that could have had with him taking Marcy off somewhere."

"And that was hours ago," Lila objected. "Why aren't they back? Unless—" her voice broke, "something's happened to them—"

"Now, Lila, don't get excited." Dad sounded somewhat excited himself. "There must be some logical explanation—"

Ken said glumly, "I better go down and tell the others she's not here."

"We'll all go down," Mom said determinedly. "Bring your friends in, Ken. They're anxious, too. And maybe some of them will have some idea about Marcy." She told her husband, "You'd better get dressed, George. You may have to go somewhere, do something. If there's been an accident—there *are* a lot of accidents, you know—" she caught her lip hard between her teeth.

"Now, Mom," Ken put a comforting arm around her shoulders, "don't go figuring there's been an accident."

"Yes, but why would they leave the club like that and not come back—unless—" Mom's anxious glance went to Dad and she asked, "George, just how much do you know about this man Bonner?"

"Well—" Dad looked unhappy, "not too much. The Chicago personnel office will get around to sending me his full record eventually, but they haven't yet."

"Oh," Mom moaned, "and we let Marcy go out with him—"

"Now, Lila," Dad soothed, "he's been living here with us. You know he's all right."

"I know nothing of the sort," Mom said, as they all went downstairs. "I took your word for it that he was the sort of person we should have under our roof—and you know nothing whatever about him! How could you have been so negligent, George?"

Ken slipped out to bring in the others.

"This is ridiculous," Dad was saying as they all filed miserably into the living-room. Mom sat huddled on the couch, while Dad prowled back and forth in front of her like a caged lion. He insisted, "I'm sure Bonner wouldn't just—kidnap her."

"Maybe," Mom moaned, "he was in some kind of trouble. That wire— Or they could both have been hurt in an accident."

"You know," Liz said reflectively, "I'll bet they *did* elope."

"Elope?" Mom's mouth dropped open just a little.

"Well, you know how sort of romantic Marcy is," Liz said. "And Jerry Bonner's older and terribly attractive to women."

Rosemary nodded. "My sister says every girl at the plant—"

Ken silenced her with a look. "Marce has got too much sense for that," he insisted.

Liz said, "Yes, but she had this quarrel with Steve. Maybe on the rebound—"

"Now, look," Steve said in a strangled tone, "don't go blaming it on me!" He appealed to Ken, to the older Rhodeses, "You know how I feel about Marcy. Why,

I wouldn't do anything to hurt her for— And anyway, we've had scraps before. She knows we'll make up again, the same as I do."

Mom spoke in the most determined voice Ken had ever heard her use. "I think this has gone far enough. George, call the police."

"The police?" Dad repeated, appalled. "But, Lila, think what that'll mean for Marcy if—"

The sound of a car approaching stilled the words on his lips. Everyone sat arrested, listening, as it drew nearer. When it turned onto the drive, seven individually held breaths were expelled in an audible sigh of relief.

"There!" Dad said triumphantly. "I knew we were getting all worked up over nothing. I knew it! . . ."

No one said a word until Marcy stood in the living-room doorway, staring astonished at the assembled company.

Then Mom got up and hurried to her, gathering her close in her arms for a shaken, speechless moment.

"Well, for pity's sake," Marcy said. "What's the matter? What's everybody doing here?"

"Waiting," Dad said in a thunderous voice, "for you! Where's Bonner?"

"Out in the car," Marcy said. "It looked like you were having a party, so I told him I'd come in first and explain things and see what you want him to do."

"Want him to do!" Dad exploded. "It seems to me he's

already done plenty. Young lady, your mother and I have been worried to death about you. So has Ken—everyone," he made a wide encompassing gesture. "You've got a lot to explain!"

"I don't see why you're all so excited," Marcy said plaintively. "You don't know about a thing yet."

"We know you and Jerry simply disappeared from the dance," Mom said sternly. "And you've been gone hours and hours without letting us know—"

"I didn't know you'd be worried," Marcy broke in earnestly. "I didn't think we'd be gone so long, but Elaine's train was late."

"Elaine?" several questioning voices repeated.

"Mrs. Bonner," Marcy said. "Jerry's wife."

"Oo-oo-oh," Mom said weakly and sat down hard on the couch.

"You see," Marcy said, "Jerry got a wire from her. She said she'd arrive on the eleven o'clock train in Clay City. And it was after ten-thirty when the wire came, so he had scarcely time to get there—we didn't know then that the train would be so late. So I had to go along to show Jerry all the short cuts, so he could make it in time. But I thought we'd be back long before anyone missed us."

Dad barked, "What's all this about Bonner's wife? I never knew he had a wife."

"Neither did I," Marcy admitted, with a little smile, "till tonight." She was proud of that smile. The news that

Jerry was married had come as quite a blow to her. Not for worlds would she have admitted how stunned and hollow she had felt all the time he was explaining the unusual circumstances of his situation. Nor how numbness had gripped her all during the drive to Clay City. It surprised her a little to realize that she was capable of smiling even now. She went on, "You see, Jerry and Elaine have only been married a year. And—well, I guess she's always been sort of under her family's thumb, or that's how Jerry felt anyway. So when he was transferred to Westfield, he figured it would be a wonderful chance to get Elaine away. But naturally, her folks didn't want her to leave Chicago, so they worked on her till Elaine refused to come here with Jerry. She wanted him to stay in the city and get another job. He got mad and she got mad, too. He said he was coming and she could do as she pleased—so she went home to her parents. That's why Jerry's been so unhappy all the time. Can you blame him?"

"I blame him for not telling us he was married," Dad said. But his voice wasn't quite so thunderous as it had been.

"Still I can see his position," Mom said. "If she wouldn't come with him—well, I suppose he didn't know just how to explain the situation. I suppose he figured, as long as we didn't ask—"

"That was just it, Mom," Marcy said. "He didn't know

what to do. So he just let things drift, hoping Elaine would change her mind. And, sure enough, she did. She missed him as much as he's been missing her, so she decided to leave her folks and come here and—that's all there was to it."

"Isn't it romantic?" Liz breathed ecstatically.

And Rosemary sighed, her eyes shining, "Oh, yes."

Steve snorted.

Marcy looked at him inquiringly. "Why, Steve. What are you here for?"

"Because—because—" Steve flushed. "Oh, skip it."

Mom said, "But, Marcy, you say they're out in the car now, both of them?" And then, at Marcy's nod, "Well, let's get them in, for pity's sake."

"They wanted to wait," Marcy explained, "in case you'd rather Jerry took her to the hotel."

"Oh, no," Mom said.

And Dad added, "Of course not! That hole would be enough to break them up all over again." He chuckled. "Now she's here, I'll bet they find a place of their own in a hurry. I'll go right out and tell them to come in."

Marcy's glance met Steve's a little shyly. After all, she thought, he must have been worried about her, or he wouldn't be here. The knowledge made a little glow of warmth around her heart, enough to melt the remaining hurt of her disappointment over Jerry. Maybe, she told herself, hurts like this were a part of growing up.

Steve's glance was steady on hers, his lips twisted into a not too willing grin.

Ken said, "You know what, kids? We were all in such a hassle over Marcy, we forgot to have our regular after-the-dance hamburgers. I'm starved."

"I'll fix some," Mom offered, getting to her feet. "Seems to me we all need sustenance."

Among the murmur of assent, Steve's voice was most enthusiastic of all as his fingers closed around Marcy's.

The End

Printed in Great Britain
by Amazon

19270731R00129